The PAINTBOX Project

Elizabeth Bruce and Judy Jarvis

Acknowledgements

Written by Elizabeth Bruce and Judy Jarvis

Illustrated by Wendy Carolan

Cover design by Jane Taylor

The ecumenical group responsible for this Activity Club material consisted of:
Elizabeth Bruce, National Christian Education Council
Anne Dunkley, The Baptist Union
Judy Jarvis, The Methodist Church
Rosemary Johnston, The United Reformed Church
Steve Pearce, The Church of England
Valerie Stephens, Sheffield Christian Education Council

The publishers gratefully acknowledge permission to reproduce the following material, but if any rights have inadvertently been overlooked, the necessary correction will gladly be made in subsequent editions.

The extract from *Growing in Faith* is reproduced by permission of Lichfield Diocesan Board of Education.

'I had a paintbox' by Tali Shurek, from *My Shalom, My Peace* (Sabra Books, Tel Aviv). Permission sought.

'Calming the storm' from *Feeling Good!* by Peter Churchill (National Society/Church House Publishing) is copyright © Red Lentil Music 1994 and is reproduced with permission of the publishers.

The Universal Prayer for Peace. Permission sought.

'Just a tiny seed' (Music by Tracy Atkins; words by Richard Atkins and Andrew Pratt) Words and music © 1995 Stainer & Bell Ltd, London, England and The Trustees for Methodist Church Purposes (UK). Reproduced from *Big Blue Planet* by permission of the publishers.

'The Pines' by Margaret Mahy from *The First Margaret Mahy Story Book* is reproduced by permission of J M Dent, London.

'God, Father of all' from *Prayers for a Fragile World* is reproduced by permission of Lion Publishing, Oxford.

'Questions' by Wes Magee (from *The Witch's Brew & Other Poems* by Wes Magee, Cambridge University Press, 1989) is reproduced with permission.

'What is red?' from *Hailstones and Halibut Bones* by Mary O'Neill, copyright © 1961 by Mary LeDuc O'Neill, is reproduced by permission of Egmont Children's Books Ltd, London and Doubleday, New York, a division of Random House, Inc.

The extract from *Values and Visions* is reproduced by permission of Manchester Schools Improvement Services.

'The love of God' (music by Sylvia Crowther) music © 1995 Stainer & Bell Ltd, London, England and The Trustees for Methodist Church Purposes (UK). Reproduced from *Big Blue Planet* by permission of the publishers.

'O what a wonderful world' (Words and music by Estelle White) © Kevin Mayhew Ltd, Buxhall, Stowmarket, Suffolk IP14 3BW. Used by permission.

Published by:
National Christian Education Council
1020 Bristol Road
Selly Oak
Birmingham
Great Britain
B29 6LB

British Cataloguing-in-Publication Data:
A catalogue record for this book is available from the British Library.

ISBN 0–7197–0965–2

First published 2000
© 2000 National Christian Education Council

Designed and typeset by Avonset
Printed and bound by Ebenezer Baylis, Worcester, UK

Contents

Introduction 5

Wonderful White 13

Beautiful Blue 21

Gorgeous Green 31

Yippee Yellow 37

Radiant Red 43

Brilliant Black 48

Resources:

Administration: forms etc. (photocopiable) 52

Templates (photocopiable) 54

Songs 58

Information for Portrait of the Artist 65

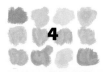

INTRODUCTION

Why The Paintbox Project?

Think of a world without any colour! *The Paintbox Project* is about exploring and celebrating our world and our faith. It aims to enable groups to:

- ◆ Enjoy doing things together.
- ◆ Share experiences of life and faith.
- ◆ Celebrate specific colours as part of God's colourful creation.
- ◆ Remember aspects of Jesus' ministry and the life of the Early Church through stories in Luke and Acts.

Biblical background

Each session focuses on a particular colour, linking it to a particular theme. Although there is a good deal of Christian material and thinking here, *The Paintbox Project* is written for everybody, whether they have close links with the Christian community or not.

The sessions are:

- ◆ *Wonderful White* — the Holy Spirit comes on Jesus at his baptism.
- ◆ *Beautiful Blue* — Jesus brings peace and calm into difficult situations.
- ◆ *Gorgeous Green* — Jesus uses his experience of the natural world in his teaching.
- ◆ *Yippee Yellow* — Jesus uses stories to help people understand.
- ◆ *Radiant Red* — the Spirit breaks down barriers.
- ◆ *Brilliant Black* — the Christian community celebrates.

The final session, *Brilliant Black*, contains suggestions for drawing everything together, whether in worship or in some other way that is appropriate to your group or situation. You could also involve the rest of your church and/or members of the wider community.

Educational principles

The Paintbox Project has been written with a number of educational principles in mind:

- ◆ Meaningful learning starts from the individual's experience.
- ◆ Involving the whole person is the most effective way of learning.
- ◆ Variety of activity gives everyone the opportunity to take part.
- ◆ Being part of a community is important.
- ◆ A sense of security is vital for learning.
- ◆ Having fun is part of experiencing God as love.

The material in this book has been written so as to be suitable for all kinds of groups: children's holiday clubs, church weekends, after-school clubs, all-age weekends away, Lent groups and any other context you care to dream up. Most of the suggestions are suitable for a wide age-range.

You are not expected to do everything: it is for you to decide what is suitable for the group of people with whom you are working and to select and adapt accordingly. More material is provided for each session than could possibly be used, so that you can choose what suits your needs. The built-in flexibility means that *The Paintbox Project* can be used equally well by groups of any size: you do not need huge numbers in order to have a good event.

The Paintbox Project — How?

Who gets involved?

All those taking part in *The Paintbox Project* are referred to as Painters. In each session there is the opportunity to look at a picture, find out about famous painters, discover a different way of using paint and make a large picture or collage. In these and other ways, Painters focus on the different colours which play such an important part in our world.

Getting started

The Paintbox Project will need long and detailed planning, and will benefit from you adding your own ideas, knowing what will work in your group and situation. Gather together a group to plan how you will use *The Paintbox Project*. Group planning has many benefits, including the stimulation of a wide range of ideas, the pooling of resources and the sharing of responsibility.

- The planning group should set realistic aims for the Project. The sessions can then be planned to create opportunities for Painters to achieve those aims. At the end of the Project you can ask yourselves, 'To what extent were the sessions successful in achieving the aims?' For a group unused to working together, it may be appropriate to work to a general aim such as, 'To provide Painters with an experience of learning from each other.' In another situation your aim would probably be more specific.

- Most of the activities suggested can be led by people who do not usually lead educational work but have appropriate skills. Remember that people of all ages have skills to share.

- Every group is made up of individuals who learn in different ways and at different speeds. Be careful to ensure that a variety of styles is used, and that all parts of the programme are based on active participation in order to increase the opportunities for everyone to learn. This is even more important with all-age groups.

- Allow space for reflection. One way of doing this is to talk about what you have done together. A quiet time around a focal point might offer another opportunity for reflection which all ages can enjoy together.

- Stories are accessible to all ages. Adults and children alike gain much from stories, and it is worth investing time in your story preparation. An episode of *Luke's story* is included in each session. It will be useful to plan ahead and ask an individual or a group to take responsibility for it, encouraging the use of any musical, dramatic or dance skills.

- The environment in which you meet can help or hinder the learning of your group. Try to make your meeting-place as comfortable and as attractive as possible. Use anything appropriate to set the scene: pictures and posters can be collected in the weeks beforehand. For each session you will need a large copy of a painting. Think about any pictures, posters and so on that you have on your walls at home. They don't have to be religious!

- A group learns as it goes. Learning is related as much to the opportunities for Painters to talk to each other during the session, as it is to the tasks they are given. Activities should therefore be relaxed in style and there should be plenty of opportunities for people to talk about what they are doing and learning.

- If it is appropriate for your group to have times of prayer, plan something slightly different for each session. Prayer needs variety and participation. Try to involve Painters in ways other than listening.

- Enjoyment is important and motivates people to join in. Give opportunities for letting off steam as well as more obviously purposeful activities!

All-age groups

Learning in all-age groups is valuable for everyone. Children and young people come to know and appreciate attitudes and values which adults wish to pass on but find difficult to express in words. Adults can be reminded of Jesus' teaching that we should have child-like qualities such as trust and openness. A child's viewpoint can often challenge adults to reconsider their attitudes.

Today more and more churches are using all-age approaches to worship and learning. Whether you have experience of this or not, here are a few hints to assist in the planning and leading of all-age groups.

'The "all-age" experience takes place when —

◆ a group of people of various ages, including both adults and children, meet together for a common purpose;

◆ it is recognized that everyone has a contribution to make from which others can learn;

◆ the activity encourages people to reflect on their experience and share it with others so that everybody can learn from it;

◆ the people leading see their role as helping and encouraging this process rather than teaching.'
(from *Growing in Faith*, Lichfield Diocesan Board of Education, 1990)

◆ Since everyone is a learner when it comes to organizing all-age events, the planning and leading are usually best done by a group rather than by an individual. People of all ages should be involved in that group. Bear in mind the need to plan for sessions in which everyone learns and everyone contributes.

◆ Review your planning and consider how each session or day will be for a 5–year-old, for a 9–year-old, for a 50–year-old, and so on!

◆ There are many people in our communities who have learning difficulties. There are also many who experience considerable loneliness, especially during holidays when some facilities are closed. An all-age event is an ideal occasion for all sorts of people to join in, so why not make sure there are one or two extra helpers, and make an effort to involve everyone?

What you will get out of *The Paintbox Project* depends on you and the other Painters, and what you all share and do together. A purposeful, confident group can be created by planning carefully, paying attention to the well-being of individuals and generating a loving atmosphere within which the group can enjoy themselves.

Organization: Colour Groups

The Paintbox Project uses small Colour Groups as the basis of its organization. Decide how many groups you will need. A good size for a working group is between six and ten people, but you should decide on group sizes according to your own needs and circumstances.

How you form groups will also be affected by your needs and circumstances. It may be appropriate for these groups to be all-age: there are many activities within *The Paintbox Project* which are suitable for all-age groups. However, it might be more appropriate in some situations for each group to be for a particular age-group so that activities can be more narrowly targeted. Each group should have a co-ordinator who has been involved in the planning of the Project.

Planning the sessions

In each session, activities appear under a number of headings:

Preparing the studio gives ideas for setting up the room where you will meet. Each time, the colour is important, so use it as creatively as you can. This need not cost a lot of money if you use resources that are already to hand.

Getting geared up suggests activities for the Painters to do when they arrive.

◆ *Paintbox passes* have to be prepared and filled in.
◆ *Making your gear* involves making something to wear.

Getting into the picture

◆ *Today's painting* focuses on a particular painting of your choice. Sample questions are given as discussion starters.
◆ *Portrait of the artist* focuses on the person who painted the picture. Information about some artists is given on pages 65–69. Add

information from other sources, such as reference books or the Internet. Again, sample questions are given as discussion starters.

Artists' antics

- *Colour Group collage* is an activity for the group whose colour is the focus of the session.
- *Painting:*
  - *Paint the theme*
  - *Play with paint* introduces different techniques using paint.

  Crafts

  Team games:
  - *Treasure hunt* can be done out of doors, if the weather and your situation permit.

Painters' pantry

- *Recipes*
- *Snazzy snacks*

Find out, in advance if possible, whether any members of your group (leaders as well as Painters) have food allergies or special dietary requirements, such as diabetes, the coeliac condition, an allergy to nuts, sensitivity to food colourings. Be sure to provide alternative foods so that no one feels excluded. It is also important that those who are responsible for serving the food know exactly what ingredients are in each dish so that they give the right advice to anyone who asks.

It should go without saying that all food must be prepared and stored in line with current health and hygiene guidelines.

Finding the focus

- *Stories,* including Luke's story
- *Worship:*
  - *Action*
  - *Songs and prayers*

You are not expected to use all the material provided for each session. You will need to choose what is appropriate for the group of people you are working with. For *The Paintbox Project* to work well, you will need to start planning in good time. Begin early with outline plans, and add in more

detail as you go along. Here are some guidelines for planning and preparation.

Choosing a leadership team

- Many hands don't just make light work, they make better work too.
- A new Project is an opportunity to involve some new people.
- As well as leaders and helpers, think of specific tasks that individuals might be invited to do, such as acting, cookery, collage, photography, publicity. A list on pages 10–11 suggests some of the roles which might be needed.
- Follow the Home Office *Safe from Harm* guidelines, or check your organization's or denomination's guidelines on the protection of children and the appointment of leaders. If you do not have a copy of the guidelines, contact your organization's or denomination's regional office or national headquarters.
- Your leaders and helpers will be grateful for any training you can arrange. Again, contact the regional or national office of your organization or denomination for information about courses and training events.

This book is full of ideas, a number of which will fire your imagination and suit your group. It is important that all who will have leadership roles have an opportunity to look through the material before your first planning session, so that they come fired with enthusiasm for what they would like to do.

Agenda for Planning Meeting 1

- What is your target group? What age-range do you want to attract?
- What are you aiming to achieve? Write it down for future reference.
- Where and when will you hold the sessions? Don't just assume that your local church buildings will do! The venue will

need to have a large communal space, enough room for the number of people you hope to involve, an area suitable for messy activities, and adequate toilet and washing facilities. It also needs to be maintained to a standard which is safe for activities which involve children.

- What facilities are needed for each age-group and each activity? Do you need special facilities such as ramps, and wheelchair access to toilets?

- What is your organization's policy for selecting and screening those who work with children?

- Does your group's existing insurance policy include this sort of event, or will you need to take out separate cover?

- Inform the local authority's social services department if children under eight are to be present for more than two hours at a time. You will need to register with your local social services if you will meet on more than six days in the year.

- Brainstorm initial ideas, using the material as a basis.

- Plan a general framework for the sessions, including an outline timetable.

- Decide how many people you will need to run the event and identify who else could be asked to become involved.

- Where and how will you publicize *The Paintbox Project*? Who will be responsible for this?

- Prepare a budget for both income and expenditure. Will you ask Painters to pay something towards the costs? Are there other sources of income you could tap?

Agenda for Planning Meeting 2

- Make a list of leaders and helpers.
- Make sure that you have a qualified First Aider.
- Check your organization's policy guidelines for work with children and decide how to deal with any requirements you have not yet met.

- What needs to go on registration/consent forms? (See example on page 53.)

- Are you going to ask people to register in advance?

- How will you allocate the Painters to groups? Will it be on the basis of age or interest, for example?

- Which activities will you do in each session?

- Make a list of all the equipment and materials you will need, and allocate responsibility for acquiring them.

- How will you approach the final session, *Brilliant Black*?

Agenda for detailed planning meetings

Plan each session in detail:

- For each activity within each session, who will do what, when and where?

- Which activities will be done in Colour Groups, which in other groupings, and which with everyone together?

- What materials are needed and how are they being obtained?

- How will you register attendance each day? Who is responsible for this?

- Do any of the Painters have special needs or medical requirements? How will these needs be met?

- Arrange a site meeting for all leaders and helpers at least a week before the club will begin, to check:
  - that people know which groups they will be working with;
  - that everyone knows what they are responsible for;
  - what needs to be done to prepare the building beforehand;
  - where each activity will be held;
  - that all equipment is in good working order;
  - that you all know where the fire exits are, where the nearest telephone is, and so on.

Personnel

To run *The Paintbox Project* effectively, you will need a large number of helpers. Here is a list of possible jobs. Which ones will you need? Try to get a good mix of ages and genders amongst your helpers.

Art and Craft Organizer(s)

If possible, find someone who has expertise and experience in arts and crafts, to provide both ideas and support for those who are less experienced. This person could also be responsible for identifying other people with a particular gift or interest which they might be willing to offer on a one-off basis to the Project. You will need to decide who will be responsible for ensuring that all necessary materials are available — either this person or the individual group leaders.

Caretaker

Although everyone should share responsibility for clearing up at the end of sessions, it is generally helpful to appoint someone to co-ordinate this and ensure that it is done.

Catering Team

These people will provide refreshments in each session. They may also supervise and help with cooking activities.

Games Organizer(s)

It is best if you can find someone with experience and skill in organizing games to take on this role.

Health and Safety Officer

If you cannot find someone with a current First Aid certificate to take on this responsibility, send someone on a training course beforehand. They should be present throughout all sessions of the Project. They will need to check that the First Aid box is well stocked and that any items used are replaced immediately.

Interior Designers

A team of people who are responsible for preparing the room or building before each session will lessen the load on those who are in charge of the activities. Imaginative use of the colour for the day will enhance the session and stimulate the Painters' creativity.

Musician

It can be helpful to have someone to take responsibility for music in the sessions, particularly to teach the Paintbox Song (see page 58) and any other new songs. The person does not have to be an instrumentalist; it is more important that they are good at leading and at giving others the confidence to sing and play.

Publicity Officer

You will need someone with creative flair to make and distribute posters, publicity flyers and invitations. They should also liaise with the local press and any visitors to the event. Even if your local newspaper is not willing to send a photographer, they may well be pleased to publish a photograph and short article supplied by your Publicity Officer.

Secretary

Appoint someone to be responsible for all paper-work. It is helpful to have someone to take notes at planning meetings and to write any letters that may be required. Easy access to a photocopier is a distinct advantage. It is particularly important to have help with collecting and filing registration forms at the first session of the Project, if this has not been done in advance.

Story-teller

You will need someone who can do justice to the stories, especially if they are to be told to the whole group. Whether stories are read or told is less important than the way in which it is done.

Treasurer

It helps if one competent person is responsible for all money matters, including collection, counting, banking, paying bills and keeping accounts. Specific duties such as collecting money from Painters may be delegated to others if you wish.

Welcomers

These people will welcome Painters when they arrive and help them to find their way around if necessary. They will also be on hand to help anyone who is struggling, to be alongside children during activities and to be a listening ear when needed.

Worship Leader

If you want to include a time of worship in each session, it will be helpful to have someone who will take responsibility for the smooth running of this part of the programme. If they are able to circulate during the session, they can link the worship to the activities, discussions and so on.

Running each session

Making a good start

- ◆ Make sure that all leaders arrive in good time — at least 30 minutes before the session is due to begin.
- ◆ Go through the plans for the session together, checking that there are no questions or misunderstandings and that everyone has the necessary equipment.
- ◆ Have people in place to register Painters as they arrive and others on hand to involve them in activities straight away.

Keeping on track

There are four main elements to bear in mind in each session:

Aim

Keep in mind the overall aim you have decided on for *The Paintbox Project*, but have a clear aim for each session too. You should feel free to adapt the suggested aims which are printed at the start of each session.

Needs

Think about the people who will take part. What do you think they need? What do they think they need? What do they enjoy? What are they able to do? How can you give them the confidence to try new things?

Plan

Choose activities which are suitable for your group and which will help to achieve the aim(s) you have set. Write out a plan for the session (see the planning sheet on page 52).

Time

Draw up a timetable for each session. Even if you do not keep to it strictly, you will at least have thought about whether your plan is realistic or not.

Agenda for a follow-up meeting

It is a good idea to have a follow-up meeting to review the Project while it is still fresh in everyone's minds.

- How did it go?
- What worked well?
- What could be improved on?
- What did the Painters think of it?
- Do you want to keep in touch with the Painters? If so, how?
- What do you want to tell your organization or church:
  → about the Project?
  → about future work and events?
- Who will report to whom, and how?
- Do you want to recommend *The Paintbox Project* to others, or send comments to the publishers, NCEC?
- What would you need to bear in mind if you were to hold a similar event on another occasion?

WONDERFUL WHITE

Aims:

- ♦ To recognize the significance of new beginnings.
- ♦ To celebrate white as part of God's colourful creation.
- ♦ To remember Christ's baptism and the coming of the Holy Spirit as a dove.

Preparing the Studio

Hang white streamers (made from crêpe paper) and white balloons across the room.

Prepare the materials, equipment and rooms for the activities.

Getting geared up

Paintbox Passes

See the template on pages 54–55 .

Issue *Paintbox Passes* to Painters as they arrive. Provide a white sticker to attach to the Wonderful White space in each Pass.

Group badges

Provide each Painter with a badge showing the colour of their group.

13

Making your gear: Hats

You will need a selection from the following, all in white:

- paper (tissue, crêpe, cartridge, for example)
- card
- wool, lace, tape, ribbon
- paper doilies, paper plates
- scraps of fabric
- cotton wool balls
- scissors, Copydex, PVA glue, staplers, sticky tape

Use the materials to make hats.

Why not have a fashion parade to admire each other's creativity?

Getting into the picture

Today's painting

Ask some appropriate questions, such as:

- Do you like this picture? Why/why not?
- What does it say to you?
- How old do you think this painting is? What makes you think this?
- Why do you think the artist painted it?

Portrait of the artist

Again, ask some appropriate questions, such as:

- What can you tell about the artist from the picture?

- How do you think the artist was feeling?
- What do you think the artist was trying to say?

Share some information about the artist, using the material on pages 65–69 or from other sources.

Colour Group

Encourage the White Group to make a collage of a white dove over water. Provide a range of materials, such as: tissue paper in whites, blues and greens; metallic paper; feathers.

Artists' antics

Painting

Paint the theme

Do a painting to illustrate new beginnings.

Play with paint: Squeezy painting

You will need:

- flour
- salt
- white poster paint
- icing bags and nozzles or small plastic squeeze bottles (for example, washing-up liquid bottles)
- thick paper or thin card in strong colours
- silver glitter (optional)

Mix equal parts of flour and salt. Add paint to form a paste. Pour into icing bags/bottles. Squeeze the paint onto the paper to make a design or pattern. If you wish, sprinkle glitter over the paint while it is still wet, to make it sparkle.

Crafts

Hanging doves

You will need:

- white card or thick paper
- thinner white paper
- thread
- scissors
- dove template (page 56)

Use the template to cut a dove shape from the white card. Cut a slit along the dotted line. Fold the thinner paper into a fan. Push the 'fan' through the slit to form the wings. Attach the thread so that the dove can be hung up.

Dove kite

For each kite you will need:

- A3 card or thick paper
- 2 drinking straws
- glue (optional)
- stapler, scissors
- hole punch and hole reinforcing rings
- paper or plastic streamers
- thin string
- dove kite template (page 57)

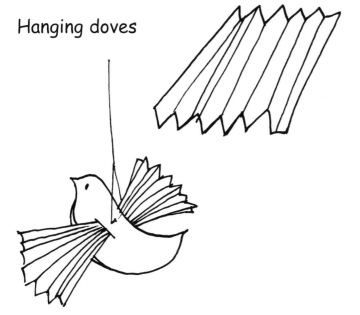

15

Fold the card in half and use the template to cut a double dove shape from it. Place one drinking straw inside the fold, and glue or staple the two halves together as far as the dotted line. Staple the other drinking straw to the wings in such a way as to hold the wings back. Staple on the streamers to form the tail. Punch a hole in the body and strengthen it with the reinforcing rings. Thread string through the hole. If the weather conditions are suitable, go outside and see how well your dove flies.

Weaving

Experiment with weaving white strips in different textures. Depending on your circumstances, experience and confidence, you can choose to make a large wallhanging, adding to it as you focus on each colour. Alternatively, you can make individual pieces of weaving and put them together at the end of the Project.

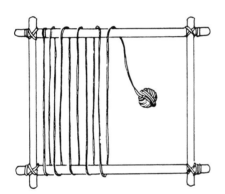

For a large wall-hanging you will need:

- lengths of dowelling or 4 long garden canes
- thick string
- strips of a variety of fabrics and other materials such as wool, raffia, hessian, paper, plastic

Tie the canes together and wrap the string around them to form warp threads (see the diagram above). Weave the fabrics and so on in and out of the warps. When the weaving is finished, display it without removing it from the 'loom'.

For individual weaving you will need:

- white card (other colours for other days)

- strips of different kinds of paper (for example, crêpe, foil, sugar paper), ribbon, plastic

Fold the card in half and rule lines on it, stopping short of the outer edge (see diagram 1). Cut along the lines. Open out the card. Weave the strips of paper and so on (the wefts) in and out of the slits in the card (the warps). Experiment with altering the spaces between the warps, by either leaving different amounts of space between the slits or cutting sections out of the card (see diagram 2). A different effect can be achieved by using different widths and textures for the wefts, or cutting them in wave shapes. If you weave the wave-shaped strips in the same order as you cut them out, they will fit together.

①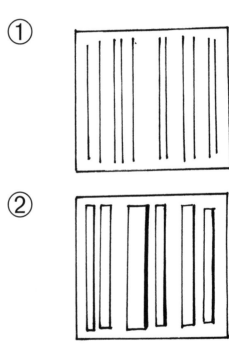

②

③

Wonderful White

Plaster pot stand

For each person you will need:

- ◆ a plastic or strong cardboard lid, at least 10cm in diameter
- ◆ plaster of Paris, mixed to a thick creamy consistency
- ◆ small marbles/fine gravel/shells/pebbles

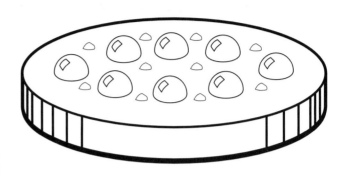

Half-fill the lid with plaster of Paris. Decorate with gravel or whatever, making sure that the top is level. Leave to set.

Team games

Table tennis ball races

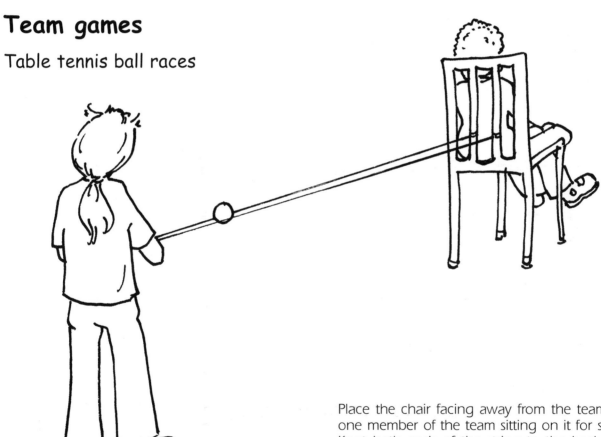

For each team you will need:

- ◆ a wooden-framed upright chair (or suitable substitute)
- ◆ a table tennis ball
- ◆ a 4–metre length of smooth string

Place the chair facing away from the team, with one member of the team sitting on it for stability. Knot both ends of the string to the back of the chair, about 3–4cm apart.

Take it in turns to hold the string away from the chair with two fingers, forming two parallel 'tram' lines. Roll the ball along the 'tram' lines until it touches the back of the chair. Then allow it to roll back down. If the ball falls through the lines or over the back of the chair, the go must be repeated. Continue until everyone has had a turn.

Flour game

You will need:

- a bowl, and a plate with a larger diameter than the top of the bowl
- enough flour to fill the bowl to the brim
- a knife and spoon
- small sweets, such as chocolate drops
- a plastic table cloth or groundsheet to protect the surrounding area
- a towel

Spread the table cloth on the floor. Fill the bowl with the flour. Make sure the flour is firmly packed, and turn it out onto the plate. Carefully place a sweet on top of the flour 'mound'. The group should sit or kneel in a circle round it. In turn, each person takes the knife and slices off a part of the mound. The person who causes the mound to collapse must pick up the sweet with their teeth. They will then need the towel to clean their face! Collect the flour into the bowl and repeat the process until everyone has had a go at retrieving the sweet.

Treasure hunt: Colour search

Challenge each Colour Group to see how many different white objects they can find outside, within a specified time limit. Each object must be of a different material, for example stone, flower, plastic.

 # Painters' pantry

Microwave meringues

You will need (makes 40):

- 1 egg white
- 250–350g icing sugar, sieved

Break up the egg white lightly with a fork and then work in as much icing sugar as possible. The amount of sugar will depend on the size of the egg. Work the mixture together with your hands until it is dry and can be kneaded. If it is too sticky, add a little more icing sugar; if it is too dry, add a drop or two of cold water. Knead well.

Divide the mixture into 40 pieces about the size of marbles. Arrange 6 in a circle on baking parchment/greaseproof paper, spacing them out so that the meringues can spread. Cook, uncovered, in the microwave for about 1 minute, until risen and firm. Place on a wire rack to cool. Cook the remaining meringues 6 at a time.

If preferred, the meringue mixture can be put into paper cake cases and cooked 8 at a time for about 1¹/₄ minutes.

Macaroon bars

You will need:

- 1 dessert spoon cold mashed potato
- 450g icing sugar
- melted chocolate
- coconut (can be toasted if you wish)

Mix the potato and icing sugar. Roll out to about 1cm thick. Melt half of the chocolate and use it to coat the top of the potato mixture. Sprinkle coconut on top. Once the chocolate has hardened, turn the bar over and coat the other side with chocolate and coconut.

Snazzy snacks

- cream cheese on crackers
- cream cheese roll-ups (made with bread)
- lychees & banana chunks on sticks

Serve on white plates with white serviettes.

Finding the focus — New beginnings

New experiences

Gather all the Painters into the middle of the room. Point to two walls which are opposite each other, as you give the following instruction (or similar): 'If you were born in this town/village/country, run to this wall; if you were born in another town/village/country, run to that wall.' Then point to the other two walls of the room, as you give the following instruction (or similar): 'If you have ever moved house, run to this wall; if you have always lived in the same house, run to that wall.' Continue in the same way with these instructions:

'If you have changed school...; if you have always gone to the same school...'

'If you have a baby under 2 in your family...; if you do not have a baby in your family...'

'If you have grown a new tooth recently...; if you have not...'

'If you went on holiday to a new place last year...; if you did not...'

Add to or adapt these instructions to suit the group.

Doing things differently

Set these challenges:

- ◆ Cross the room individually with no feet touching the floor.
- ◆ Cross the room in pairs, using only two legs.

Spider's web

You will need:

- ◆ a large ball of string

Stand in a circle. One member of the circle holds the end of the string and throws the ball to someone else. As they do so, they say their own name. The catcher holds on to the string and throws the ball to another person, saying their own name as they do so. Continue until everyone is part of the web.

Stories

(either all together or in Colour Groups)

Use either or both of these stories and the accompanying questions, to suit your situation.

Harry's story

Harry was the class thief. In his class at school, whenever anything went missing, it was Harry who had taken it — scissors, sweets, chocolate bars, packed lunches, favourite toys. You name it, Harry took it! His teacher was at the end of her tether, the other children were angry and Harry was very miserable. The more miserable he became, the more things he stole.

The time came for Harry to move to a new school where nobody knew him, but his old teacher warned his new teacher that Harry was a thief. On his second day there, a pair of scissors went missing.

'We need a detective,' said the teacher. 'Who's got sharp eyes and is good at looking for things? What about you, Harry?' Harry led the search and, after a few minutes — surprise, surprise! — he had found the scissors. From then on, when something occasionally went missing, Harry was in charge of the search and almost always found the missing object. Harry was no longer the class thief; he was the class detective!

Talk together about the story, using these questions and any others that may arise:

♦ Do you think the new teacher was right to ask Harry to be the class detective?

♦ What can we do to help people make a new start?

Luke's story

Read or tell Luke 3.18, 21–22. Talk together about the story, using these questions and any others that may arise:

♦ What new things are happening in this story?

♦ Why does this story matter?

Song

Learn the first verse of the Paintbox Song (see page 58) and sing it several times.

Action

Those who made doves can collect them and hold them during the prayer.

Prayer

God of new beginnings, thank you —

for the new friends we've made today;
for the new things we've done together;
for the new ideas we've shared.

God of new beginnings, thank you —

for creating us;
for forgiving us through your Son, Jesus;
for sending us your Spirit, coming like a dove.

Amen

BEAUTIFUL BLUE

Aims:

- ◆ To recognize our responsibility to be peacemakers.
- ◆ To celebrate blue as part of God's colourful creation.
- ◆ To remember that Jesus brings peace and calm into difficult situations.

 ## Preparing the Studio

Hang blue streamers and balloons across the room.

Prepare the materials, equipment and rooms for the activities.

 ## Getting geared up

Paintbox Passes

Issue Paintbox Passes to Painters as they arrive. Provide a blue sticker to attach to the Brilliant Blue space in each Pass.

Making your gear: Ties

For one necktie you will need:

- wrapping paper, approximately A4–sized, in shades of blue if possible
- round elastic
- scissors, glue

Fold the wrapping paper as shown in diagrams 1–5. To make the knot, cut a rectangle of wrapping paper. Fold in the edges and glue it to the top of the tie. Cut a length of elastic and feed it through the 'knot'. Tie the ends of the elastic together.

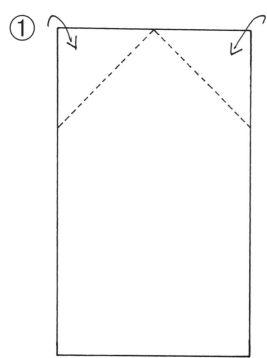

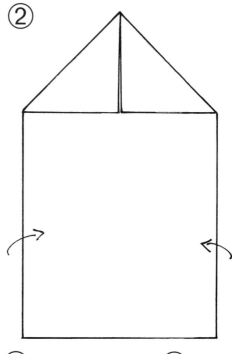

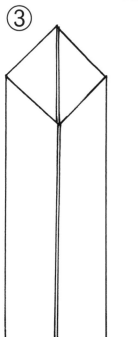

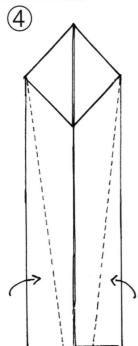

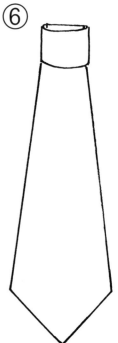

Beautiful Blue

For one bow tie you will need:

- ♦ blue crêpe paper
- ♦ round elastic
- ♦ scissors, glue

Cut a piece of crêpe paper measuring 25cm x 10cm. Glue the ends together to form a ring.

Cut a narrow strip of crêpe paper. Shape the ring into a bow by squeezing it together in the centre.

Wind the narrow strip around the middle to hold it in shape and glue it in place.

Thread a length of elastic through the 'knot' and tie the ends together.

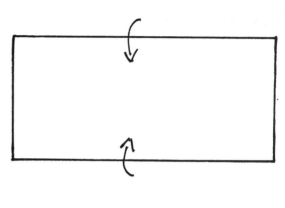

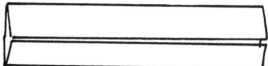

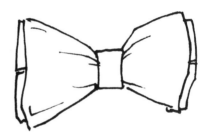

Getting into the picture

Today's painting

Ask some appropriate questions, as on page 15.

Portrait of the artist

Again, ask some appropriate questions, as on page 15. Share some information about the artist, using the material on pages 65–69 or from other sources.

Colour Group

Encourage the Blue Group to make a collage of a sailing boat, waves and sky. Provide a range of materials, such as: paint (particularly blues and greens), tissue paper, silver paper, brown paper, fabrics in shades of blue and white.

The Paintbox Project

 # Artists' antics

Painting

Paint the theme

You will need:

- paper of different sizes
- a range of paints, particularly blues
- paintbrushes and so on

Read this poem to the group:

> I had a paintbox —
> Each colour glowing with delight;
> I had a paintbox with colours
> Warm and cool and bright.
> I had no red for wounds and blood,
> I had no black for an orphaned child,
> I had no white for the face of the dead,
> I had no yellow for burning sands.
> I had orange for joy and life,
> I had green for buds and blooms,
> I had blue for clear bright skies,
> I had pink for dreams and rest.
> I sat down
> and painted
> Peace.
>   (*Tali Shurek, aged 13*)

Paint pictures illustrating peace.

Play with paint: Marbling

You will need:

- metal roasting pan or deep tray
- paper
- oil-paints in shades of blue
- white spirit
- paintbrush

Half-fill the tray with cold water. Thin a little oil-paint with white spirit and dot it onto the surface of the water with the brush.

Hold a sheet of paper by two opposite corners and pull it gently across the surface of the water. Lay it aside to dry.

Experiment with different effects by adding two or more shades of paint to the water. Use the end of the paintbrush to move the colours around before lowering the paper onto the surface.

To clean the water in order to achieve a different effect, skim the paint off the surface with scrap paper.

Crafts

Paste sculptures

You will need:

- card (for example, cereal packets)
- thin galvanized wire
- newspaper
- cold-water paste mixed to a thick creamy consistency
- J-cloths or equivalent

Make figures of Jesus and his disciples, using these instructions.

Beautiful Blue

①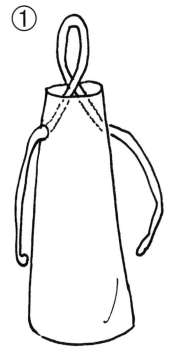

Make a cone from cardboard. Trim the bottom edge so that the cone will stand properly. Cut a length of wire (about 60cm) and insert it into the cone, forming the neck and arms.

②

Bend back the ends to make hands. Crumple a ball of newspaper for the head and push the wire 'neck' into it, securing it with strips of pasted newspaper.

③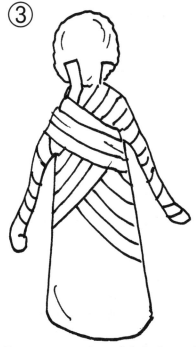

Cut or tear strips of J-cloth and dip them in the paste one at a time. Squeeze out any surplus paste, then wind the strips around the hands, arms and upper body.

④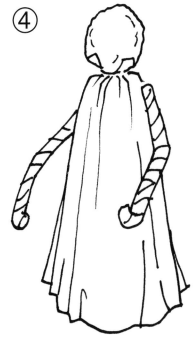

Take another J-cloth, dip it in the paste, squeeze it and drape it around the figure. Push the arms through the J-cloth and arrange the extra fabric in folds. Bind at the neck with strips of J-cloth.

⑤

Cut a square of J-cloth for each sleeve. Fold each into a triangle, soak it in paste and arrange it around one of the arms. Cover the face with a small J-cloth square, then use a rectangle of J-cloth to make the headdress.

Leave to dry in a low oven. The figures can be painted if you wish.

25

The PAINTBOX Project

Paper boats

You will need:

♦ one square of paper for each boat.

①

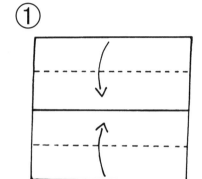

Fold the paper in half and open it out again. Fold the top and bottom edges to the crease.

②

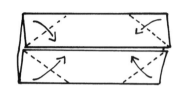

Fold the four corners inwards.

③

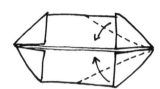

Fold in the corners at the right, as if making a paper aeroplane.

④

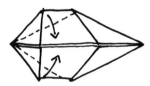

Repeat with the corners at the left, overlapping the creases made in step 3.

⑤

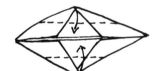

Fold in the top and bottom corners to the centre crease, pressing firmly.

⑥

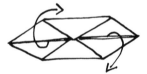

Open out all the layers, revealing the base inside.

⑦

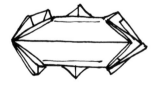

This forms a loose boat shape. Turn it over.

⑧

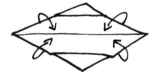

To lock the boat, push down on the corners and turn the whole structure inside out.

⑨

Try sailing the boats!

26

Beautiful Blue

Hands across the world

You will need:

- ◆ a large circle of blue paper (for example, sugar paper)
- ◆ different shades of blue paper (can be wrapping paper)
- ◆ glue, felt-tipped pens, scissors

Roughly draw the outline of the continents on the blue circle. Draw round each other's hands on the different shades of blue paper, and cut them out. Stick on the hands so that they span the globe.

Weaving

If you are making a large wall-hanging, add blue strips in different shades and textures.

If you prefer to do individual weaving, follow the instructions given on page 16.

Team games

Flip the kipper

For each team you will need:

- ◆ a fish shape cut from an A4–sized piece of paper
- ◆ a newspaper or magazine

Line up the teams at one end of the room. When the starting signal is given, the first person in each team should run to the other end of the room and back, using their newspaper as a fan to 'flip' the kipper. (Note: this is the only legitimate way to make the kipper move!)

When they arrive back at their team, they hand the newspaper to the next person, and so on.

The first team to finish is the winner.

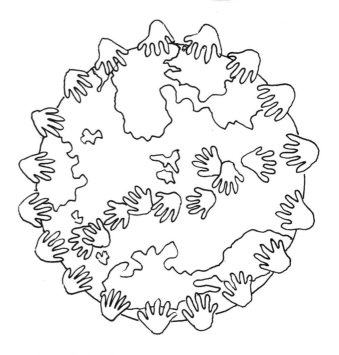

Wee Jimmie

You will need:

- ◆ a story involving as many characters as there are in each team, and/or a quick-witted story-teller

Line up the teams at one end of the room. Each team member is allocated the name of a character in the story. This can be either a person (for example, 'Mr Smith' or 'the mother') or some other character (for example, 'the lion' or 'the duck'). Make sure that Wee Jimmie is included. If not all teams have the same number of people, some team members will need to take on more than one character.

As the story is told, team members should listen out for mention of their character. When it is mentioned, they should run to the other end of the room and back to their place.

From time to time, mention several characters together (for example, 'Wee Jimmie, his mum and his dad' or 'all the animals in the zoo').

It is virtually impossible to keep score, so it is best to play this just for the fun of it!

Treasure hunt: Letter search

Challenge each Colour Group to see how many objects beginning with B they can find outside, within a specified time-limit.

Drama: Stilling the storm

Either:

Tell the story of Jesus calming the storm (Luke 8.22–25). The disciples were enjoying their boat trip across the lake after a busy and exciting day. Jesus was asleep when a storm blew up and huge waves crashed over their small boat. The disciples rushed to wake Jesus up; they were terrified that the boat would sink. Jesus said to the sea, 'Hush! Be still!' and the waves calmed down, and the sea became peaceful and smooth.

Talk about the disciples' feelings during the storm and later when all was calm.

Act out the story. A long strip of blue material with someone holding each end and waving it up and down can give a most effective stormy/calm impression. (A blue sari would be ideal.) The other Painters can act out the disciples' fear and then relief.

Or:

Learn 'One day when we were fishing' (see page 60), with all the actions. If you wish, use a strip of blue material as described above.

 # Painters' pantry

Coconut ice balls

You will need:

- 150g desiccated coconut
- 300g icing sugar
- 4–5 tablespoons evaporated milk
- blue food colouring

Mix coconut and icing sugar. Add evaporated milk and a drop of blue colouring. Mix to a stiff consistency, adding food colouring until the desired shade is achieved. Knead until smooth. Shape into balls and leave to set on a plate dusted with icing sugar.

Crystallized flowers

You will need:

- violets, lilacs or borage flowers (the flowers must be fresh, dry and in perfect condition)
- 250g caster sugar
- 1 egg white

Spread some sugar on a plate and put some more into a small sieve. Break up the egg white with a fork, but do not whip it. Remove the stems and any leaves from the flowers. Paint each flower lightly all over with egg white, then lay it on the plate of sugar and sprinkle more sugar over it. Coat all the flowers in sugar in this way, one at a time.

Then lay them on baking sheets lined with grease-proof paper and dry them for 24 hours in a barely warm oven, turning them several times during the first few hours. They will keep for up to a year. (Note: other types of flower can be crystallized in the same way, but make sure that they are safe to eat before serving them. Inedible flowers can be kept safe and used for display if you prefer.)

Snazzy snacks

- blueberry jam sandwiches/roll-ups
- blue icing on biscuits
- blue sweets, for example M&Ms
- blue milk-shake/ice cream soda

Serve on blue plates with blue serviettes.

Finding the focus —
Peace, perfect peace

Listening

This may be best done in Colour Groups. Use these or similar instructions:

Sit in a comfortable position and relax. Block your ears with your thumbs and cover your eyes with your hands. Count ten breaths, then bring your hands gently down to your lap.

Once everyone is ready, talk about what people heard and anything else that they noticed.

Now use these or similar instructions. Pause where there are dots.

Sit in a comfortable position and relax ... Listen carefully to the sounds around you ... Sounds that are far away ... Sounds that are near you ... Loud sounds ... Quiet sounds ... Concentrate on your sense of hearing ... Now I will count slowly to five; when I reach five, open your eyes. One, two, three, four, five.

If you feel it appropriate, share experiences of doing this.

Back to back

Sit on the floor, back to back with a partner. The aim is to stand up, using only the force of each other's body to do this, and then to sit down again.

- ◆ What do you learn from this about co-operation?

Home rules

You will need:

- ◆ pen/pencil and paper for each group

Divide into groups of three or four. If possible, put people of different ages in each group. Ask each group to think up at least five rules for the home and look at them from different points of view:

- ◆ What would an under-five-year-old want?
- ◆ What would an eight-year-old want?
- ◆ What would a thirteen-year-old want?
- ◆ What would a parent want?
- ◆ What would a grandparent want?

Note: the ages can be varied to suit your situation.

- ◆ Compare and discuss the results. What needs to happen if the rules are to be fair for everyone?

Stories

(either all together or in Colour Groups)

Use either or both of these stories to suit your situation.

Sean's Story

(read or tell)

On Saturday 15 August 1998, a bomb exploded in the centre of Omagh, in Northern Ireland. One of the people killed was an eleven-year-old boy called Sean McLaughlin. Not long before that, he had written a poem expressing his optimism that the signing of peace accords was finally bringing peace to his country. Here is his poem:

The Bridge

Orange and Green — it doesn't matter
United now
Don't shatter our dream
Scatter the seeds of peace over our land
So we can travel
Hand in hand across the bridge of
Hope.

- ◆ What does this poem say to you about peace?
- ◆ What are your hopes for the future and how would you express them?

The PAINTBOX Project

Luke's story

Ask the drama group to act out the stilling of the storm (Luke 8.22–25) or to sing the song 'One day when we were fishing' (page 60). Sing it through a second time, with everyone joining in.

- ◆ What does this story tell us about Jesus?
- ◆ What does it say to us here today?

Song

Learn the second verse of the Paintbox Song (see page 58). Sing the song from the beginning.

Painting peace

Read the poem 'I had a paintbox' to the whole group. Ask those who painted pictures of peace to show their paintings and talk about them.

Action prayer

You will need:

- ◆ a low table covered with a dark blue cloth
- ◆ a silver tray, cake base or hoop
- ◆ strips of crêpe paper or strands of wool in light blue and dark blue, enough for everyone to have one of each; attach to the underside of the tray with sticky tape
- ◆ a cross and an oil lamp with blue oil, or a blue candle
- ◆ quiet, reflective music: for example, *Canon* by Pachelbel, or *Air in D Major* (Air on a G string) by Bach, or *Meditation* from *Thaïs* by Massenet

Note: if you have a large number of Painters, you may prefer to do this in Colour Groups.

Light the candle or lamp. Ask each person to hold the free ends of a dark blue strip and a light blue one. Use the following ideas to encourage reflection while the music is playing:

- ◆ Focus on your dark blue strip and think about yourself — things you find hard and things you find easy.
- ◆ Focus on your light blue strip and think about other people — those you like and those you don't like.
- ◆ Twine your two strips together and think about ways in which you can make friends — make peace.

Song

Peace, perfect peace *(Rejoice & Sing)*

Prayer

(This Universal Prayer for Peace is used by many people all over the world at midday every day)

> Lead me from death to life,
> from falsehood to truth.
> Lead me from despair to hope,
> from fear to trust.
> Lead me from hate to love,
> from war to peace.
> Let peace fill our heart,
> our world, our universe.
> Peace — Peace — Peace

Reverently lay the strips down.

GORGEOUS GREEN

Aims

- To share concern for the natural world.
- To celebrate green as part of God's colourful creation.
- To remember that the seemingly small and insignificant has a part to play in God's world.

Preparing the Studio

Hang green streamers and balloons across the room.

Prepare the materials, equipment and rooms for the activities.

Getting geared up

Paintbox Passes

Issue Paintbox Passes to Painters as they arrive. Provide a green sticker to attach to the Gorgeous Green space in each Pass.

Making your gear: Bracelets

To make one pipe-cleaner bracelet you will need:

- 3 pipe-cleaners, in shades of green if possible
- several beads

Thread the beads onto one of the pipe-cleaners. Twist all three pipe-cleaners together about 3cm from one end.

Plait or twist them, as evenly as possible, leaving about 3cm free at the other end. Make it into a bracelet by twisting the ends together.

To make a safety pin bracelet you will need:
- safety pins of uniform size
- small beads, in shades of green if possible

Thread beads onto the safety pins. Link several safety pins together to make a bracelet. Experiment!

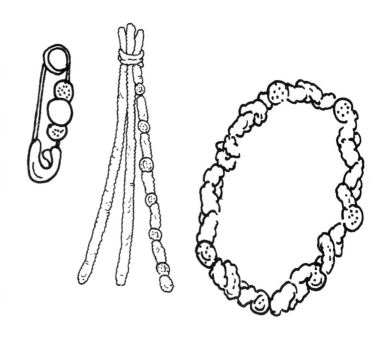

Getting into the picture

Today's painting

Ask some appropriate questions, as before.

Portrait of the artist

Again ask some appropriate questions. Share some information about the artist, using the material on pages 65–69 or from other sources.

Colour Group

Encourage the Green Group to make a collage of a tree. Provide a range of materials, such as leaves, bark, seeds and grasses. Paint diluted PVA over the leaves in the completed collage to prevent them from curling up.

Artists' antics

Painting

Paint the theme

Do a painting to illustrate concern for the natural world.

Play with paint: Bubble painting

You will need:
- washing-up liquid
- powder paint in different shades of green
- drinking straws
- paper
- empty yoghurt pots

Gorgeous Green

Pour ¼ cup of washing-up liquid into a yoghurt pot. Mix a small amount of water with powder paint and add it to the washing-up liquid until a strong colour is obtained. Blow through a straw into the paint mixture until the bubbles slightly overflow the container.

Roll a piece of paper lightly around on top of the bubbles so as not to burst them. Do not press the paper flat on top of the bubbles. Repeat the process with several different shades.

Crafts

Plate garden

For each pair you will need:

- ◆ a large plate or small tray
- ◆ compost/soil
- ◆ fine gravel and larger stones (can be gathered outside)
- ◆ moss
- ◆ cress or mustard seeds
- ◆ small twigs, pieces of bark
- ◆ small bedding plants or seedlings or cacti

Note: these items can vary according to your situation.

Give each pair the freedom to design and assemble their own garden.

Green 'flower' arrangement

You will need:

- ◆ a variety of containers
- ◆ green oasis
- ◆ either a range of greenery or, if appropriate, secateurs to enable Painters to gather their own outside

Cut the oasis to fit the container and add water. Create an arrangement with the greenery.

Weaving

Add green strips in different shades and textures.

Rubbish sculptures

You will need:

- ◆ a collection of 'clean' rubbish: for example, boxes, cardboard tubes, yoghurt pots, polystyrene packing, bubble wrap, ice lolly sticks, scraps of cloth, wool, wrapping paper
- ◆ sticky tape, strong glue, scissors, stapler

Give Painters permission to use the materials to create whatever they like.

Team games

Dried pea race

For each team you will need:

- 2 saucers
- 10 dried peas (fewer for younger children)
- a drinking straw per person

Put each team's peas on a saucer and place it beside an empty saucer on the floor. Line up all the saucers at the opposite end of the room from the teams. If any team members are unable to kneel down, put the saucers on tables.

Give each person a drinking straw.

Team members in turn run to their saucers and transfer all the peas from one saucer to the other by sucking through the straw. (Note: this is the only legitimate way of moving the peas!) Any peas which fall on the floor (or table) must be retrieved using the straw.

The first team to finish wins.

Crackerjack quiz

You will need:

- a low chair or stool for each contestant
- a range of prizes which can be shared out in a Colour Group (for example, a bag of crisps, a bag of potatoes, a bunch of grapes, a box of crayons, a packet of biscuits, a comic)
- green balloons, blown up

Have a quiz in which each Colour Group provides a contestant. Each of them must stand on a low chair or stool.

Contestants are given a 'prize' to hold each time they answer a question correctly. Each time they answer wrongly or drop an object, they are given a green balloon. (Note: balloons must NOT be held by the knotted end.)

At the end of the quiz, contestants are allowed to keep all the items they are holding and share them with their Colour Group.

Treasure hunt: Nature search

Challenge each Colour Group to see how many different kinds of leaves they can find within a specified time-limit.

Drama: How rubbish took over the world

Talk about what it would be like if rubbish took over the world. Work together to improvise a short piece of drama on this theme.

 # Painters' pantry

Chervil soup

You will need:

- 3 handfuls of chopped fresh chervil or 3 tablespoons dried chervil
- 3 tablespoons butter or olive oil
- 2 rounded teaspoons flour
- 100ml cold water or stock
- 500ml hot stock
- salt and black pepper to taste
- 1 tablespoon cream (fresh or sour)

Sauté the chervil in the butter/oil. Add the flour and sauté again. Slowly add cold water/stock and stir to a smooth consistency. Add the hot stock, salt and black pepper and simmer for 20 minutes. Remove from heat, add cream and serve.

Peppermint creams

You will need:

- 500g icing sugar
- ¼ teaspoon cream of tartar
- evaporated milk
- peppermint essence
- green food colouring
- additional icing sugar to dredge
- walnut pieces (optional)

Sieve icing sugar and cream of tartar. Add enough evaporated milk to mix to a stiff paste; add flavouring and colouring as desired. Knead the mixture, using icing sugar to prevent sticking. Roll out to a thickness of approximately 1cm and cut into circles or any other shapes. Moisten the top with evaporated milk and decorate with walnut pieces.

Snazzy snacks

- salad of dried fruit, including figs
- fresh figs
- green salad

Serve on green plates with green serviettes.

Finding the focus — God's world

Planting

Transplant seedlings from trays into individual pots (which the Painters can take home and care for). If possible, go outside and plant seeds or a young tree.

Guided meditation: Just a tiny seed

This may be best done in Colour Groups. Use these or similar instructions. Pause where there are dots.

Sit in a comfortable position and relax … Let your feet rest flat on the floor … Let your hands rest in your lap … If you wish, you may close your eyes while you listen.

Imagine that you are a seed in a packet of many seeds … What does it feel like inside your packet? … Is it warm or cold? … Are the other seeds good seeds or bad seeds? … How big are they? … What shape and colour are the seeds? … Is it comfortable to be with the other seeds, or are you longing to escape? … Now imagine that the packet is being opened, and the seeds are being shaken into the earth … Imagine you are falling

from the packet and are landing in the rich, dark, moist earth ... It is soft and damp all around you and it gets darker as you are covered over. How do you feel? ... Comfortable? Uncomfortable? ... What does it smell like? ... What can you hear? ... Imagine that the warmth and moistness have touched your seed skin ... Your skin is softening and swelling, and your outer jacket has slowly split ... Something exciting is happening ... Slowly, gently, feel the roots poking out from your feet, roots stretching and reaching and spreading, looking for more soft, moist soil, sucking up the water and food into your body ... Now, imagine the first shoots emerging from your hands; gradually stretching and reaching upwards ... The soil feels heavy and you have to push quite hard ... Bend your head and use your shoulders to push ... If you wish to look up now, you will see a crack of light just above you ... You are very near the surface now; just one last effort and you will break through. Just take a deep breath and push ... Your shoot has just broken through the surface of the soil and you can see the sun for the first time. How do you feel? ... Imagine yourself unfurling, slowly, as you stretch out your leafy arms to the sunlight, and turn your face to feel the warmth of the sun's rays... How do you feel? ... What can you smell? ... What can you hear? ... You may go on growing for a few moments ... What kind of seed are you and what are you growing into? ... When you are ready, open your eyes and look around you.

Luke's story

Read the parable of the mustard seed (Luke 13.18–19).

- ● Why do you think Jesus told this story?
- ● What do you think it says to us today?

Song

'Just a tiny seed' (see page 61). Have a leader sing each line, which is then echoed by the Painters.

What can we do?

Ask those who made rubbish sculptures to show them and talk about them.

- ● How are we spoiling our world?
- ● What can we do about it?

Poem: *The Pines*

Hear the rumble,
Oh, hear the crash.
The great trees tumble.
The strong boughs smash.

Men with saws
Are cutting the pines —
That marched like soldiers
In straight green lines.

Seventy years
Have made them tall.
It takes ten minutes
To make them fall.

And breaking free
With never a care,
The pine cones leap
Through the clear, bright air.

   (*Margaret Mahy*)

- ● What does this poem tell us about God?

Song

Learn the third verse of the Paintbox Song. Sing the song from the beginning.

Prayer

God,
Father of all,
Creator of clean waters,
blue skies, of sparkling snow
and yellow wheatfields.
Forgive us the waste we dump,
the forests we destroy,
the greyness we create.

   (*Emoshioke Imoedemhe [age 11]*)

YIPPEE YELLOW

Aims

- ♦ To recognize the importance of light in everyday life.
- ♦ To celebrate yellow as part of God's colourful creation.
- ♦ To remember that Jesus asks us to be lights in the darkness.

Preparing the Studio

Hang yellow streamers and balloons across the room.

Prepare the materials, equipment and rooms for the activities.

Getting geared up

Paintbox Passes

Issue Paintbox Passes to Painters as they arrive. Provide a yellow sticker to attach to the Yippee Yellow space in each Pass.

The PaintBox Project

Making your gear: Masks

Smiley sunflower

For one mask you will need:

- a paper plate
- yellow crêpe paper
- scissors, glue
- felt-tipped pens
- dried sunflower and/or pumpkin seeds (optional)
- a stick or piece of garden cane
- sticky tape

Make a frill of crêpe paper and glue it round the edge of the plate. Draw features on the face. Cut out the eyes. If you wish, decorate the face with patterns of seeds. Attach a stick to the back of the plate so that you can hold it in front of your face.

Laughing lion

For one mask you will need:

- a paper plate
- yellow paint, paintbrushes, etc.
- strips of yellow paper or gold gift-tie ribbon
- black paper
- scissors, glue
- felt-tipped pens
- a stick or piece of garden cane
- sticky tape

Paint the plate yellow. Draw on the features and cut out the eye holes. Curl strips of paper or ribbon and glue them round the edge of the plate. Add a nose and whiskers cut from black paper. Attach a stick to the back of the plate so that you can hold it in front of your face.

Friendly fire

For one mask you will need:

- a paper plate
- yellow paint, paintbrushes, etc.
- yellow and orange cellophane or paper
- scissors, glue
- felt-tipped pens
- a stick or piece of garden cane
- sticky tape

Paint the plate yellow. Draw features on the face and cut out the eye holes. Cut flame shapes from cellophane or paper and glue them round the edge of the plate. Attach a stick to the back of the plate so that you can hold it in front of your face.

Yippee Yellow

Getting into the picture

Today's painting

Ask some appropriate questions.

Portrait of the artist

Again ask some appropriate questions. Share some information about the artist, using the material on pages 65–69 or from other sources.

Colour Group

Encourage the Yellow Group to make a collage on the theme of light in the darkness. Provide a range of materials, such as: paper and fabric in shades of yellow; metallic paper; ribbon.

Artists' antics

Painting

Paint the theme

Do a painting to celebrate yellow in God's colourful creation.

Play with paint: String painting

You will need:

- lengths of string of varying thicknesses
- paint of varying thicknesses in trays or shallow dishes (mix some with PVA if wished)
- paper

Fold a sheet of paper in half then open it out. Holding both ends of a piece of string, dip it into a tray of paint. Lay the paint-soaked string on one half of the paper and fold the other half over. Press down with one hand, pulling the string out with the other. Open the paper.

Repeat with a new colour, using a different piece of string. Experiment to create different effects.

Crafts

Sunflower in a pot

You will need:

- yellow, orange and green paper
- dried seeds, pulses and/or pasta
- paper plates
- plant sticks
- flower pots filled with soil or stones
- scissors, PVA glue, sticky tape and so on.

Cut petal shapes from the paper and glue them round the edge of the plate. Glue the seeds, pasta and so on in a pattern in the centre of the plate.

When it is dry, tape the plant stick to the back of the plate. Add leaves cut from green paper. 'Plant' in a pot.

Onion skin egg dyeing

You will need:

- eggs
- brown onion skins
- 20cm squares of old cloth
- small leaves and/or rice
- rubber bands

Put several layers of onion skins on a square of cloth. Add leaves and/or rice. Place an egg on top. Add more leaves, rice and onion skins. With care, wrap the cloth round the egg and skins, securing with rubber bands.

Cook in boiling water for 30 minutes. Remove the egg from the water and leave to cool. Rub in a little cooking oil to give a shiny appearance.

Super sun

You will need:

- a large circle of firm paper or card
- broad strips of paper or card
- pasta, sunflower seeds, pulses, other collage materials as appropriate
- yellow and orange paint

To make the centre of the sun, decorate the circle with pasta and so on. If wished, cover with yellow and orange paint. Cut the strips into 'flame' shapes and paint. When dry, either glue the pieces together or retain them for use in the worship time.

Weaving

Add yellow strips in different shades and textures.

Team games

Foot-ball

You will need:

- chairs for everybody
- a ball for each team

Seat teams on chairs side by side, one team facing another. Put a ball on the feet of the first person in each team. The aim is to pass the ball along the team, using only your feet. The ball must NOT touch the floor; if it does, the team must start again.

Treasure hunt: Scavenger hunt

Challenge each Colour Group to see how many of a given list of objects they can find within a specified time-limit: for example, a used match, a sweet wrapper, a crisp bag, a small piece of wool, a shoe lace.

 # Painters' pantry

Easter bonnets

You will need:

- semi-sweet biscuits
- marshmallows
- icing
- yellow food colouring
- sugar flowers, silver balls, strips of angelica and so on for decoration

Use small blobs of icing to stick a marshmallow to each biscuit, to make a 'hat' or 'bonnet'. Add yellow colouring to the rest of the icing, adding a drop at a time until you achieve the desired colour. Cover each 'hat' with icing and decorate with flowers and so on.

Yippee Yellow

Easy-to-make cake

You will need:

- 1 cup self-raising flour
- 1 cup cornflakes
- 1 cup coconut
- 100g margarine
- 1/2 cup sugar
- icing sugar

Melt the margarine over a low heat. Mix in all the other ingredients except the icing sugar. Put the mixture into a greased sandwich tin. Smooth the surface. Bake in a moderate oven for about 25 minutes. Leave to cool then ice.

Snazzy snacks

- lemon drink
- lemon curd sandwiches
- scrambled egg
- chips, crisps
- bananas and custard

Serve on yellow plates with yellow serviettes.

Finding the focus — Lighting up the darkness

Searching in the dark

You will need:

- a means of darkening the room
- a large number of small yellow objects, such as beads, sweets in wrappers, small gold chocolate coins
- torches

Hide the objects around the room. Make the room as dark as possible. Give the Painters two or three minutes to find as many of the yellow objects as they can, in the 'darkness'. At the end of that time, issue torches so that they can find the rest.

Stories

Luke's stories

Act out the parable of the lost coin (Luke 15.8–10). Talk together about the story, using these questions and any others that may arise:

- Why does the story specially mention that the woman lit a lamp? (Houses then had only one or two very small windows: there was no glass and also the house stayed cooler.)
- Why did Jesus tell this story?
- What other stories did Jesus tell about things or people that were lost? (See Luke 15.)

Use these words (or similar ones) to introduce the reading of Luke 8.16–17:

'Imagine Jesus sitting on a grassy hillside with a crowd of people pressing close to hear what he has to say. Pretend that you are one of the crowd. Think about the look on his face as he starts to talk.'

- What expression do you think Jesus had on his face?
- How do you feel when something you have done wrong is found out?
- How can we spread the light of Jesus?

Songs

'God has given us eyes to see' (Big Blue Planet)

'Jesus bids us shine' (see page 62). Try this additional verse:

> Jesus bids us smile, with a big wide grin,
> Lighting up the darkness in this world we're in.
> Laser beams of friendship, so we must shine,
> You in your small corner, and I in mine.

'Many are the light beams from the one light' (Rejoice and Sing)

Learn the fourth verse of the Paintbox Song.

Action

You will need the sun and beams made earlier.

Gather in a circle with the circle of the sun in the centre. Give each person one sunbeam and a piece of blu-tak. After the prayer, ask everyone to fasten their beams to the sun using the blu-tak.

Poem: *What is ... the Sun?*

The sun is an orange dinghy
sailing across a calm sea.

It is a gold coin
dropped down a drain in heaven.

It is a yellow beach ball
kicked high into the summer sky.

It is a red thumb-print
on a sheet of pale blue paper.

It is the gold top from a milk bottle
floating on a puddle.

(*Wes Magee*)

Prayer

Bright, shining God,
Thank you for the sun.
Thank you for its warmth and light.

Thank you for the street lights.
Thank you for their light in the dark.

Thank you for headlights and torches.
Thank you that they show the way.

Thank you for bedside lights.
Thank you for their comforting glow.

Make us like lights.
Help us to bring warmth, light and happiness.

Amen

RADIANT RED

Aims

- To enjoy doing things together.
- To celebrate red as part of God's colourful creation.
- To remember that the coming of the Spirit breaks down barriers.

Preparing the Studio

Hang red streamers and balloons across the room.

Prepare the materials, equipment and rooms for the activities.

Getting geared up

Paintbox Passes

Issue Paintbox Passes to the Painters as they arrive. Provide each with a red sticker to attach to the Radiant Red space in each Pass.

The PAINTBOX Project

Making your gear: Plaited belt

For one belt you will need:

- 3 strips/lengths of crêpe paper, thick wool or cloth, in shades of red

Knot the 3 strips together at one end. Work with a partner, one holding the knotted end and the other plaiting the belt. Tie a knot at the other end. Cut the loose ends to make a fringe. Repeat the process, reversing roles.

Getting into the picture

Today's painting

Ask some appropriate questions.

Portrait of the artist

Again, ask some appropriate questions. Share some information about the artist, using the material on pages 65–69 or from other sources.

Colour Group

Encourage the Red Group to make a collage of flames using different textures of fabric, paper and foil.

Artists' antics

Painting

Paint the theme

Do a painting to show barriers being broken down.

Play with paint: Messy marbles

You will need:

- marbles
- paint in bowls
- shallow cardboard boxes or large lids
- paper
- spoons

Place marbles in the bowls of paint. Put a sheet of paper in the bottom of a box/lid. Spoon several paint-covered marbles into the box. Roll them around so that they leave a coloured pattern on the paper. Remove the marbles with a spoon and wash them before re-using them. Take the paper out of the box and leave to dry.

Crafts

Face-painting

You will need:

- face paints
- cleansing cream
- brushes, tissues, cotton wool and so on.

Paint each other's faces using red, yellow and orange, to create patterns such as flames or suns.

Radiant Red

Balloon sculptures

You will need:

- enough balloons (especially long ones) for each person to have several

Work in twos or threes. Blow up the balloons and create a sculpture using all the balloons that you have in your pair/group.

Keep the balloon sculptures for use in the worship.

Build a wall

You will need:

- materials for making a simulated red brick wall, for example a number of shoe boxes, cardboard egg boxes or cereal packets
- red paint, large brushes and so on.
- glue or sticky tape

Make the boxes into a wall which is strong enough to stand up and to have things written or stuck onto it, but which can be broken down without too much difficulty later on. Paint the front of the wall so that it looks like a brick wall.

Weaving

Add red strips in different shades and textures.

Team games

Assault course

Construct an assault course either indoors or outdoors, using whatever equipment is available.

Making it up
(for 2 groups)

You will need:

- 3 rugs, groundsheets or similar
- 2 chairs and a blanket
- a plank
- 3 bricks or small strong plastic buckets
- a wooden box
- a piece of rope
- 2 tribes — Colour Groups or other teams
- coloured bands or badges to distinguish the teams

Place the rugs on the floor in the middle of the room to represent islands in the sea (as shown in the diagram). On island 1, place a 'volcano' (made from the chairs and the blanket), bricks/buckets and the piece of rope. On island 2 place the wooden box. On island 3, place the short plank (not long enough to reach from one island to another).

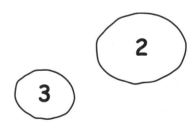

Explain that the tribe that lives on island 1 is threatened by an erupting volcano and must get off the island. The other tribe lives on island 2. Island 3 is uninhabited. The two tribes are enemies and never communicate with each other. All round the islands are shark-infested waters. Tribe 1 needs the help of Tribe 2 to escape from the volcano. The plank on island 3 may not be used directly on the water, but may be supported for example by buckets or the wooden box, which can be placed on the water.

At the end, ask the tribes what they discovered about barriers while playing the game.

The Paintbox Project

Treasure hunt: Mighty matchbox

Challenge each Colour Group to see how many different items they can fit into a matchbox within a specified time. Award 2 points per red item, and 1 point for others.

Poem: *What is Red?*

Red is a sunset
Blazing and bright.
Red is feeling brave
With all your might.
Red is a sunburn
Spot on your nose.
Sometimes red
Is a red red rose.
Red squiggles out
When you cut your hand.
Red is a brick
And the sound of a band.
Red is hotness
You get inside
When you're embarrassed
And want to hide.
Fire-cracker, fire-engine

Fire-flicker red —
And when you're angry
Red runs through your head.
Red is an Indian,
A Valentine heart,
The trimmings on
A circus cart.
Red is a lipstick
Red is a shout
Red is a signal
That says: 'Watch out!'
Red is a great big
Rubber ball.
Red is the giant-est
Colour of all.
Red is a show-off,
No doubt about it —
But can you imagine
Living without it?

(*Mary O'Neill*)

Song

Learn the fifth verse of the theme song.

Painters' pantry

Piedmontese peppers

You will need (serves 6):

- 3 red peppers
- 1 can anchovies
- 1 garlic clove, crushed
- 200g cherry tomatoes, cut into quarters
- 2 tbsp olive oil
- 2 tsp balsamic vinegar
- salt and pepper to taste

Heat the oven to 190C/Gas mark 5. Quarter and seed the peppers. Lay skin side down in a roasting tin. Cut the anchovies into 24 strips. Mix together the garlic, tomatoes, oil, vinegar, salt and pepper. Spoon some of the mixture into each piece of pepper and put 2 anchovy strips on top.

Bake for 25–30 minutes or until the peppers are tender. Leave to cool. Serve with fresh crusty bread.

Snazzy snacks

- barbecue — include tomatoes, red peppers, tomato sauce and so on
- drink ribena/red pop/red Smoothie and so on
- red jelly
- cherry cake/biscuits
- summer fruit salad — strawberries, raspberries, redcurrants...

Serve on red plates with red serviettes.

Finding the focus — Breaking down barriers

Make your own church

You will need:

- cardboard boxes of different sizes, including cereal boxes
- a large quantity of paper — different sizes and colours, including newspaper
- scissors and felt-tipped pens
- sellotape, string and paperclips

Give each collection of items to a different group: for example, cardboard boxes to the Green Group. Leave one group with nothing. Ask each group to make a model of a church. Allow 20 minutes for this activity. (Note: allow the groups to share their resources, but don't suggest it!)

Stories

Luke's story

Read or tell the story of Pentecost (Acts 2.1–18, 32, 40–41). A good re-telling of this story can be found on pages 139 and 141 of *New World* by Alan Dale (Oxford University Press).

- What barriers were broken down on the day of Pentecost?
- What difference did the coming of the Spirit make to the disciples?
- What do you think it would have been like to be there?

A teacher's story

Talk table

A teacher from Wigan writes: 'We were working on developing listening and tackling the problem of bullying. The children watched a video on bullying from the Islington Safer Cities Project.

'One idea they saw was a "talk table", a table where children who had fallen out could go and talk over what had happened. Shortly after having watched the video a table was placed outside one classroom by a teacher; on it was a notebook labelled talk table. Spontaneously children began to use the table; they would sit, talk, listen, make up by and large, or continue to feud. After using the table they entered their names and the date into the book and recorded why they had used the table and what had been the outcome. Some weeks later the children used their listening council to look at the pros and cons of the talk table. After careful consideration the children decided that they wanted to keep the table but that they themselves should think about the rules which would ensure it worked well.'

(from Values and Visions*)*

- Do you think the talk table was a good idea?
- What could you do, in your group, to sort out disagreements?

Action

Write things that divide us on the wall that you built earlier.

Prayer

Pray for forgiveness, incorporating the things written on the grafitti wall.

Action

Tear down the grafitti wall.

Ask some of the balloon sculptors to talk about the experience of working together.

Song

'The love of God' (see page 63)

OR   'The Peace of the Lord' (*Big Blue Planet*) As you sing, move around shaking hands/sharing the Peace with each other.

OR   'Break out' (*Come and Praise*)

BRILLIANT BLACK

Aims

- To share experiences of *The Paintbox Project.*
- To celebrate black as part of God's colourful creation.
- To remember that as Christians we are called to live as an inclusive community.

Preparation

- Either use the room which has been your meeting place throughout the Project or, if you are meeting elsewhere, display some of the items made by the Painters during the Project.

- In the centre of the room, if possible, place a large black circle (for example, a large dyed tablecloth).

- On the walls, display one or more 'stained glass windows', depending on the size of your group (see instructions below).

- Streamers (see below).

- Painters should come wearing clothes of their group colour and the 'gear' they have made.

Brilliant Black

Bringing it all together

Sit on the floor round the black circle.

We began *The Paintbox Project* with white. We end with black. Both colours play their part in the world of beauty and colour in which we live. Though not part of the rainbow, both are essential in helping us to see the things around us.

Poem

Black cats
Black hats
Black apes
Black grapes.

Black suits
Black boots
Black socks
Black box.

Black berries
Black cherries
Black bread
Black thread.

Black boards
Black Fords
Black bags
Black Jags.

The blacker the night
The brighter the light.

Stained glass windows

For each window you will need:

- ♦ two A1 sheets of sugar paper (or equivalent)
- ♦ black chunky felt-tipped pen
- ♦ pots of white, blue, green, yellow and red poster paint
- ♦ chunky paintbrushes

Trim one sheet of sugar paper to the shape of an arched window. Fix it to the wall and place the other sheet on the wall directly below it. Draw the outline of the 'window' with the black felt-tipped pen. Draw in the 'leading' of the window in an abstract pattern, making at least 20 areas to be filled in.

Song

Sing the first verse of the Paintbox song. Members of the White Group then place on the black cloth some of the white things made during the Project. At the same time, one member of the White Group fills in some of the spaces in the 'window' with white paint. If there is more than one window, have one Painter per window.

Proceed through the song, with each Colour Group in turn placing objects and painting spaces in the windows. By the end of the song, each window should be completely filled in.

Join →

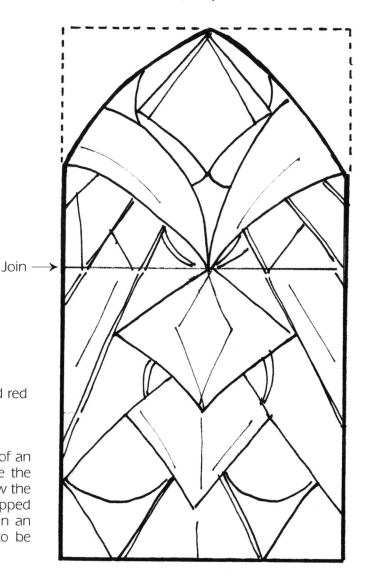

Best bits

Go into groups (either Colour Groups or others), including the visitors. Spend some time talking about *The Paintbox Project*, using questions such as these:

- What do you think have been the best bits? Why?
- What have you learned:
  - about colour?
  - about other people?
  - about God?
  - about yourself?

Thank you, God

Painting and cooking,
Talking and looking,
Reading and sharing,
Acting and caring,
Singing and eating,
Making and meeting,
Racing and playing,
Listening and praying.
Thank you, God, for all that we've done,
And the joy that's been shared amongst everyone.

Luke's story

Read or tell the story of the first Christian believers (Acts 2.42–47). A good re-telling of this story can be found on page 142 of *New World* by Alan Dale (Oxford University Press).

- Would any of this work in your situation?

Sharing

You will need:

- several bunches of black grapes, preferably seedless — enough for one grape each
- if the grapes have seeds, provide suitable receptacles for the seeds

Give out the bunches of grapes and share them around until everyone is holding a grape.

Ask everyone to look at the colour and texture of their grape, smell it and feel it, before talking to their neighbour about their reactions.

Give permission for them to eat their grapes!

- What connections can you make between this activity and Luke's story?

Song

'Round and round the circle' (*Big Blue Planet*)
As you sing, dance round the circle in the centre.

Community creed

Display the following words on a flipchart or OHP:

We believe in God.
We believe in Jesus Christ.
We believe in the Holy Spirit.
We believe in ourselves.
We believe in each other.
We believe God's Spirit works through –
Clowns and preachers,
Dogs and dandelions,
Worms and wriggly children . . .

Work in buzz groups to make up more pairs to add to this creed. Add them to the flipchart/OHP.

Streamer song

You will need:

- strips of crêpe paper approximately 30cm long x 2cm wide in white, blue, green, yellow, red, and black; enough for each person to have one

Give members of the Colour Groups their own colour of streamer. Give a mixture of colours, including black, to the visitors and helpers.

Sing 'O what a wonderful world' (see page 64), using the words below. Wave streamers of the appropriate colour during the first three lines of the verse; everyone should wave their streamers during the last line and throughout the last verse.

Brilliant Black

verse 1 O what a wonderful world!
(white streamers)

verse 2 O what a beautiful world!
(blue streamers)

verse 3 O what a gorgeous world!
(green streamers)

verse 4 O what a yippee world!
(yellow streamers)

verse 5 O what a radiant world!
(red streamers)

verse 6 O what a brilliant world!
(all streamers)

Prayer

Thank you, God, for this colourful world:
    for pale blue eyes and summer sky,
    for prickly green holly and crunchy cabbage,
    for snow-white clouds and sparkling stars,
    for glossy berries and shiny black boots,
    for bright yellow dandelions and tasty custard,
    for brilliant red rubies and glowing sunsets.
Thank you, God, for this colourful world.
Colourful God, make us more like you.
You have given us different skills and personalities.
    Together we have learned and shared,
    together we have explored your world.
Make us colourful people —
    bringing joy where there is sadness,
    hope where there is despair,
    help where there is need,
    comfort where there is loneliness.
Colourful God, make us more like you.
Amen

Song

Shalom, my friend (*Junior Praise*)

51

The Paintbox Project Session Planning Sheet

Title of Session:		Date:	
Activity		Start	Leader(s)

Materials needed	Preparation

Comments

Registration/Consent Form

The Paintbox Project is happening on:

Start time: Finishing time:

Venue: Cost:

Other details:

The person in charge of The Paintbox Project is:

Please fill in the Registration Card below and return it to me by:

Signed:

Registration Card

Yes, I would like to come to The Paintbox Project.

Name: ....

Address: ....

....

Telephone: .... Date of birth: .... School year: ......

If you are under 18, please ask a parent or carer to complete this part and sign it.

Emergency contact: .... Relationship: .... Telephone: ....

Alternative contact: .... Relationship: ...... Telephone: ....

Please note below any disabilities or medical conditions your child has (e.g. asthma, special dietary needs, regular medication). Please attach any special instructions to this form.

I have noted the arrangements for The Paintbox Project and give permission for my child to take part.

Signed: .... (Parent/Carer) Date: ....

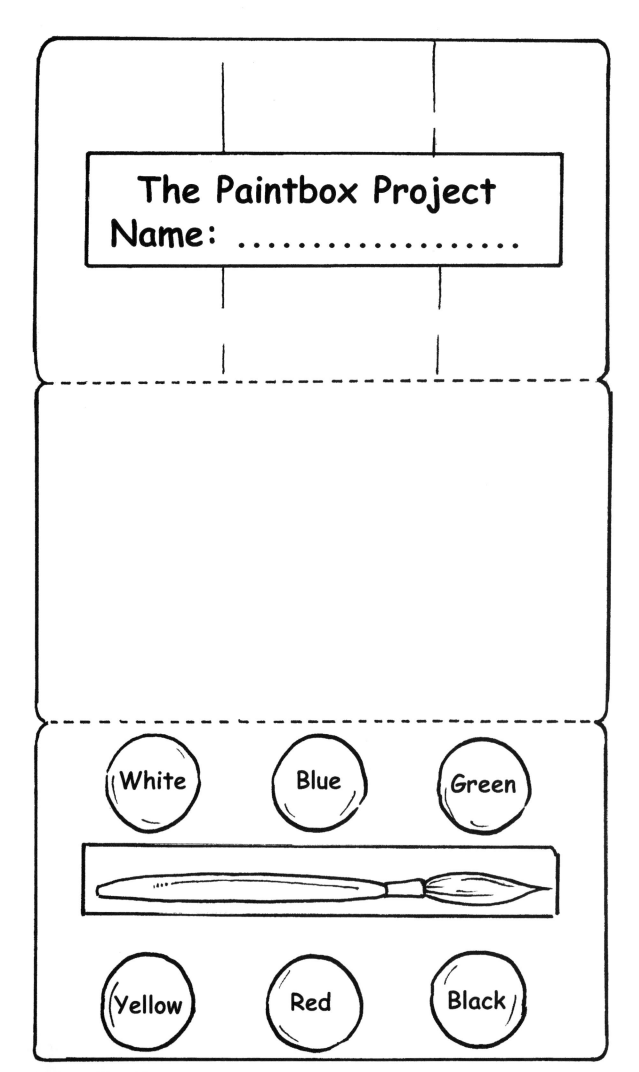

The Paintbox Project
Name: ....

White Blue Green

Yellow Red Black

My name is

. . . .

I am in the

. . . . Group

Colour data

Answer all these questions with colours.

My favourite colour is . . . .

My eyes are . . . .

My hair is . . . .

My favourite T-shirt is . . . .

My favourite food is . . . .

My favourite sweets are . . . .

My favourite football team wears . . . .

My favourite car is . . . .

My favourite animal is . . . .

My favourite bird is . . . .

My favourite weather is . . . .

Dove template

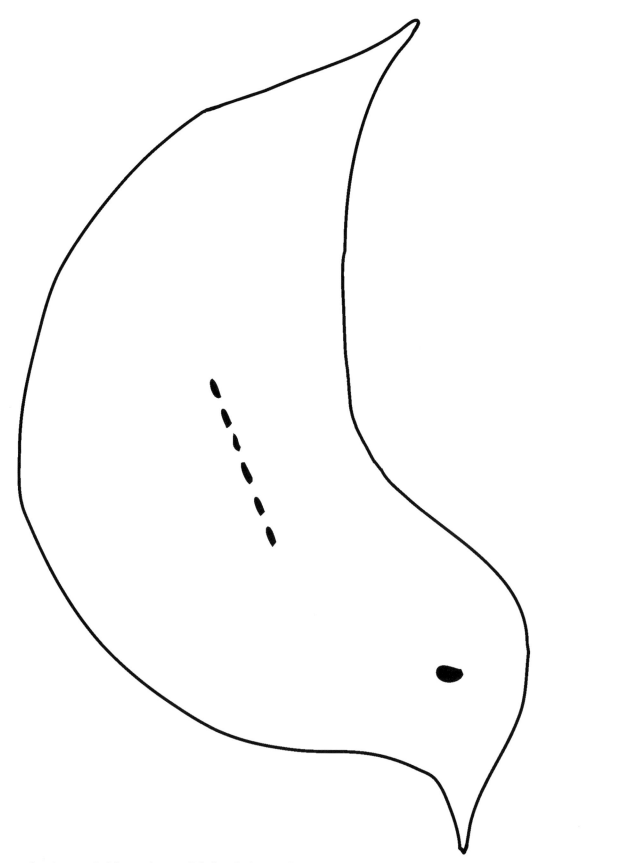

© National Christian Education Council 2000

Dove kite template

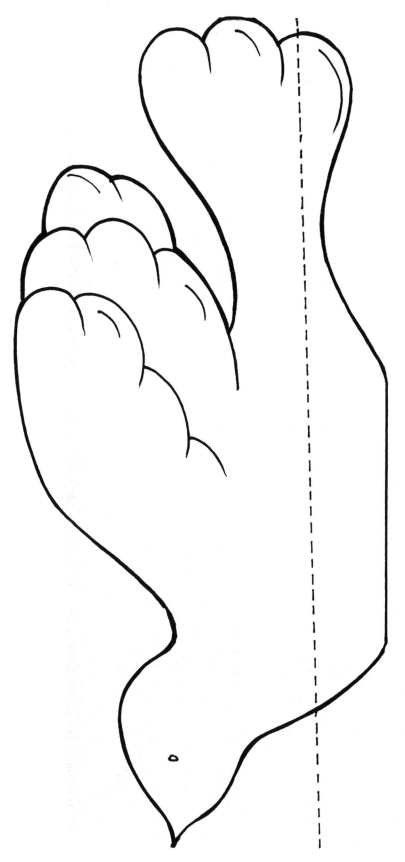

© National Christian Education Council 2000

The Paintbox Song

I'll sing you one - O   See all the co - lours - O!   What is your one - O?

One is white, a dove in flight and ev - er - more shall be so.   I'll sing you two - O

See all the co - lours - O!   What is your two - O?   Two, two, the sea is so blue,

Peace - ful and se - re - ene - O,   One is white, a dove in flight And ev - er - more shall be so!

I'll sing you three - O   See all the co - lours - O!   What is your three - O?   Three, three, the

green tree,   Two, two, the sea is so blue,   Peace - ful and se - re - ene - O,

One is white, a dove in flight And ev - er - more shall be so!   I'll sing you four - O

See all the co - lours - O!   What is your four - O?   Four for the coin so yel - low,   Three, three, the

green tree,   Two, two, the sea is so blue,   Peace - ful and se - re - ene - O,

One is white, a dove in flight And ev - er - more shall be so!   I'll sing you five - O

This page may be photocopied for use in your Paintbox Project sessions.   © National Christian Education Council 2000

The Paintbox Song (continued)

See all the col-lours-O! What is your five - O? Five for the red flames from on high and

Four for the coin so yel - low, Three, three, the green tree, Two, two, the sea is so blue,

Peace-ful and se - re - ene-O, One is white, a dove in flight And ev - er-more shall be so!

I'll sing you six - O See all the co-lours-O! What is your six - O? Six for the peo-ple shar - ing,

Five for the red flames from on high and Four for the coin so yel - low, Three, three, the

green tree, Two, two, the sea is so blue, Peace - ful and se - re - ene - O,

One is white, a dove in flight And ev - er - more shall be so!

© *National Christian Education Council 2000*

Calming the Storm

Leader   (*Speaking*) One day when we were fishing, on the lake so wide and deep,
     a storm blew up around us, but Jesus was asleep.

Children   O the waves went in and the waves went out, (*Walk in and out*)
     And the boat spun round and round. (*Turn round on the spot*)
     O the rain came down and the thunder clapped, (*Clap hands*)
     And we thought we would be drowned.

Children   (*Shouting*) Wake up Jesus!

Leader   (*Speaking*) But Jesus did not wake up.

           Children   O the waves went in ...
           (*Repeat up to 'But Jesus did not wake up'*)

           Leader   (*Speaking*) And this time Jesus did wake up...
           and clamed the storm.
           (*'Jesus' gets up and holds up his/her arms*)

           Everyone   O the waves were calm and the waves were still,
           (*Stand still*) And the boat stayed in one place.
           O the rain dried up, and the thunder stopped,
           And we knew we would be safe.

From *Feeling Good!* (National Society / Church House Publishing, 1994)
' 1994 Red Lentil Music

Just a tiny seed

Tracey Atkins (1965—

Just a ti - ny seed, In the earth it goes, Just a lit - tle

rain. It be - gins to grow.

1. Just a tiny seed,
   In the earth it goes,
   Just a little rain.
   It begins to grow.

2. From that tiny seed
   Grows a mighty tree,
   Branches spread out wide
   Shelter you and me.

3. In that mighty tree
   Birds will perch and sing.
   Like the tree, God's love
   From small seeds can spring.

Richard Atkins (1953—) and Andrew E Pratt (1948—)

Words and music ' 1995 Stainer & Bell Ltd, London, England and The Trustees for Methodist Church Purposes (UK).
From *Big Blue Planet*.

The PAINTBOX Project

Jesus bids us shine

Je-sus bids us shine with a pure, clear light, Like a lit-tle can-dle Burn-ing in the night.

In this world is dark-ness; So let us shine, You in your small cor-ner, and I in mine.

1. Jesus bids us shine
   With a pure, clear light,
   Like a little candle
   Burning in the night.
   In this world is darkness;
   So let us shine,
   You in your small corner,
   And I in mine.

2. Jesus bids us shine,
   First of all for Him;
   Well He sees and knows it,
   If our light grows dim.
   He looks down from heaven
   To see us shine,
   You in your small corner,
   And I in mine.

3. Jesus bids us shine,
   Then, for all around;
   Many kinds of darkness
   In the world are found
   Sin, and want and sorrow;
   So we must shine,
   You in your small corner,
   And I in mine.

4. Jesus bids us smile,
   With a big wide grin,
   Lighting up the darkness
   In this world we're in.
   Laser beams of friendship,
   So we must shine,
   You in your small corner,
   And I in mine.

vv. 1-3 Susan Warner (1819—1885)
v. 4 Elizabeth Bruce and Judy Jarvis

The love of God

Sylvia Crowther (1946—

The love of God
Be with you
For evermore.
Amen.

Traditional

Actions (Sylvia Crowther)
1st line: Touch right hand on left shoulder and stretch out.
2nd line: Touch left hand on right shoulder and stretch out.
3rd line: Bring hands together, palms up, into the body.
4th line: Place hands in prayer position.

O what a wonderful world

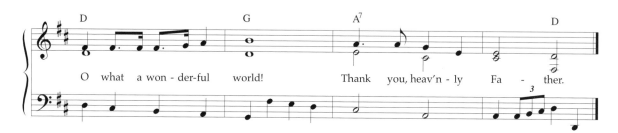

1. O what a wonderful world!
    O what a wonderful world it is!
    O what a wonderful world!
    Thank you, heav'nly Father.

2. O what a beautiful world!
    O what a beautiful world it is!
    O what a beautiful world!
    Thank you, my Lord Jesus.

3. O what a go-orgeous world!
    O what a go-orgeous world it is!
    O what a go-orgeous world!
    Thank you, Ho-ly Spirit.

4. O what a yippee-ee world!
    O what a yippee-ee world it is!
    O what a yippee-ee world!
    Thank you, heavn'ly Father.

5. O what a radiant world!
    O what a radiant world it is!
    O what a radiant world!
    Thank you, my Lord Jesus.

6. O what a brilliant world!
    O what a brilliant world it is!
    O what a brilliant world!
    Thank you, Ho-ly Spirit.

vv. 1-2 Estelle White (1925—)
vv. 3-6 Elizabeth Bruce and Judy Jarvis

Information for Portrait of the Artist

Note

All of the artists profiled here are either European or American. Do try to include artists from other cultures if possible. Good sources of Christian paintings by artists from other parts of the world are:

◆ Masao Takenaka and Ron O'Grady: *The Bible through Asian Eyes*, available from the bookshop at Churches Together in Britain and Ireland, Inter-Church House, Lower Marsh, London SE1 7EL. Tel: 020 7620 4444

◆ *The Christ we Share*, available from The United Society for the Propagation of the Gospel, Partnership House, 157 Waterloo Road, London SE1 8XA. Tel: 0207 928 8681. Also available from the Church Mission Society at the same address, and from The Methodist Church, 25 Marylebone Road, London NW1 5JR. Tel: 0207 486 5502

It is also possible to download information about artists and print out some of their pictures from the Internet.

Artists' profiles

Arcimboldo, Giuseppe (1527–1593)

Italian. One of the Mannerist painters. Famous for his 'playfully bizarre' paintings of people made up of fruit and vegetables, pots and pans, animals or workmen's tools; they were nevertheless amazingly good likenesses. Employed by several Hapsburg emperors, in Prague. Also responsible for designing decorations for festivities and designing and constructing waterworks.

Bruegel, Pieter (c.1525–1569)

Flemish. Famous for painting detailed scenes showing everyday peasant life. Paintings showed his humanistic view of the world, often with a morally didactic undertone. Applied thin layers of paint to give richness and variety of colour.

Nicknamed 'Peasant Bruegel' because he is said to have disguised himself so he could take part in peasants' gatherings.

Canaletto (1697–1768)

Italian. Famous for his paintings of Venetian landscapes, which were very detailed and much sought after by the English nobility. Visited England in 1746 and painted a group of landscapes.

Caravaggio, Michelangelo Merisi da (1571–1610)

Italian. Most important artist of the Italian Baroque. Shocked people by painting biblical scenes in powerful, realistic detail, heightened by harsh lighting and dark shadows. Wild lifestyle often got him into trouble with authority — for example, he once killed a man over a bet on a tennis match.

Cassatt, Mary (1844–1926)

American, but part of the French Impressionist movement. Specialized in painting tender scenes of everyday life, such as mothers with children. Much influenced by Edgar Degas, with whom she was closely associated. Also made extremely good woodcut prints, influenced by Japanese woodcuts.

Cézanne, Paul (1839–1906)

French. Called 'the father of Modernism'. Often painted the same scene in different lights or seasons, especially Mont Sainte-Victoire in Provence. Also did many still lifes. Used broad strokes, simple geometric shapes and bold colours. Overall design was more important to him than 'correctness' of shape or colour. Major influence on other artists, especially the Cubists.

Chagall, Marc (1887–1985)

Born in Russia but moved to France to have the freedom to paint as he wanted. Also lived in the

USA. Paintings draw on Russian folklore and his Jewish roots, which often gives them a dreamlike, magical quality. Also produced mosaics, tapestries, stained glass and other forms of art, as well as working in the theatre on set design.

Constable, John (1776–1837)

English. Romantic landscape painter. Expert at capturing effects of light, especially making the sky reflect the changeable British weather. Rivers also feature prominently, often in conjunction with scenes of rural labour. Reputed to have used 'a thousand greens' in painting landscape. Said that painting was 'but another word for feeling'. Had a strong influence on the French Naturalists and Impressionists.

Dalí, Salvador (1904–1989)

Spanish, but spent time working in Paris and New York, where he was a big star, albeit a contentious one. Belonged to the Surrealist movement. Focused on the absurd. Famous for painting dream images such as soft clocks and burning giraffes.

Degas, Edgar (1834–1917)

French. One of the Impressionists. Famous for his ballet scenes, often showing dancers rehearsing or behind the scenes in the theatre. Pictures look spontaneous as if he was merely there as an observer, reflecting his interest in photography. Fascinated by movement, shape and the harmonies of colour. Later in his life, failing eyesight made him turn more to modelling in wax; bronze casts were made after his death.

Dürer, Albrecht (1471–1528)

German, but travelled all over Europe. Regarded as one of the greatest Renaissance artists. Artist-scholar. Noted for precise observation and meticulous attention to detail. Painted many self-portraits, which was unusual at the time. Also well-known for skilful, detailed woodcuts and engravings. Revolutionized northern European art by introducing ideas from Italy. Died of a fever caught on a long expedition to the swamps of Zeeland (Holland) to see a stranded whale.

Dyck, Anthony Van (1599–1641)

Flemish. Moved to London and became a well-known portrait-painter at the English court. Knighted by King Charles I. Portraits often flattered the sitters, giving them an aristocratic bearing, refined features and long tapering fingers. Major influence on English portrait-painting.

Eyck, Jan Van (c.1390–1441)

Flemish. One of the first to use oil paints. Famous for minute detail, accurate perspective and naturalistic representation of different textures, such as skin, fabrics and animal hair.

Frankenthaler, Helen (1928–)

American. Abstract Expressionist. Pours thin paint onto huge unprimed canvases, so that the paint is absorbed ('staining'); result looks like watercolour, often giving the impression of a landscape.

Gainsborough, Thomas (1727–1788)

English. One of the most important English painters of the Rococo. Taught himself to paint. Portrait-painter but included landscape whenever possible. Wanted to free painting from stylization.

Gauguin, Paul (1848–1903)

French, but left his family and a successful career in search of a simple lifestyle on the South Sea island of Tahiti. Famous for the simple style, strong outlines, flatness and large blocks of vibrant colour in the paintings he did there. Prepared the way for Modernism.

Gogh, Vincent Van (1853–1890)

Dutch, but developed his distinctive style while living in the south of France. Post-Impressionist. Famous for his use of intense colour, hard contrasts and often heavy application of paint in which the brushstrokes can be seen. Regarded painting as the 'expression of glowing emotion'. Restless character. Had severe mental and emotional problems which led him to cut off one of his ears and, eventually, to commit suicide.

Gontcharova, Natalia (1881–1962)

Russian. Part of the Avant-garde movement in Moscow but later settled in Paris. Combined Russian folk and religious influences, including icons, with French art. Developed a primitive, fairly abstract style, before becoming an important designer for the theatre, especially of sets and costumes.

Greco, El (1541–1614)

Real name: Domenikos Theotocopoulos. Born on the island of Crete (El Greco is Spanish for 'the Greek') but, after training in Venice and Rome, spent most of his working life at the Spanish court. Famous for vigorous, usually intensely religious, paintings with swirling movement, elongated figures and bright colours. Mostly painted biblical subjects and legends of the saints.

Hockney, David (1937–)

Born in Bradford, England, but now lives in California. Hyperrealist. Typically paints scenes of swimming pools and pastel-coloured buildings. Especially interested in portraying the effect of light on water. Sometimes works from photographs, even for portraits.

Holbein, Hans (1497–1543)

German, but moved to England and became official portrait-painter to the court of Henry VIII. Sometimes included objects and symbols in his paintings to give information about the sitter. Died of the plague, in London.

Hunt, William Holman (1827–1910)

English. Co-founder of the Pre-Raphaelite Brotherhood. Showed every detail as accurately as possible. Concerned to represent moral and social values in contemporary Victorian life. Actually finished very few paintings.

John, Gwen (1876–1939)

Welsh, but spent much of her life in France. Had an unhappy liaison with the sculptor Rodin, which almost made her end her own artistic career. Tended to paint individual women with an air of loneliness and melancholy. Quiet, reclusive, died unrecognized.

Kauffmann, Angelica (1741–1807)

Swiss. Began her career as a portrait-painter at the age of 11. Moved to London where she became well-known for her portraits and mythological paintings. Also painted murals for Robert Adam and other designers, often on classical themes.

Leonardo da Vinci (1452–1519)

Italian. Regarded as a genius and the prototype of the creative Renaissance man. An innovator in painting and also a designer, musician, inventor and scientist. Completed only a small number of paintings, but many drawings and sketchbooks have survived.

Lowry, L S (1887–1973)

English. Worked as a rent collector, then as a clerk; painted as a hobby. Specialized in depicting large numbers of people set in the industrial landscape of northern England. Human figures always thin and dark, often bent and scurrying, as if unaware of their surroundings and intent on their destination.

Matisse, Henri (1869–1954)

French. Loved vivid Mediterranean colours. Chief among the Fauves (wild animals), so called because of the primitive savagery of their style. Often ignored the rules of perspective in favour of the inner harmony of the picture. Saw art as 'a comfort to the soul, something like a good armchair'. Towards the end of his life, experimented with spectacular paper collages.

Michelangelo (1475–1564)

Italian. Expert in painting and sculpting the human body, for which he studied anatomy. Probably most famous for his paintings on the ceiling of the Sistine Chapel in the Vatican; took four years, lying on his back on wooden scaffolding. Also a celebrated sculptor, poet and architect.

Mondrian, Piet (1872–1944)

Dutch, but lived in London for two years then moved to New York. Constructivist. Began painting from nature, particularly focusing on an apple tree; introduced a grid of lines which gradually took over in a series of pictures, until the tree disappeared altogether. Famous for his abstract paintings of vertical and horizontal lines and pure colours. Mostly used the primary colours red, yellow and blue, and the non-colours black, white and grey.

Monet, Claude (1840–1926)

French. Leading Impressionist. Concentrated on the effects of light and shade, especially outdoors. Worked quickly to capture particular qualities of light before they vanished. Especially famous for a series of paintings of water-lilies in his garden at Giverny.

Morisot, Berthe (1841–1895)

French. Pupil of Edouard Manet (who later became her brother-in-law). Often exhibited alongside the Impressionists, but had her own feminine delicacy of style. Tended to paint scenes of tenderness with subtle harmonious colours and delicate brushwork.

O'Keeffe, Georgia (1887–1986)

American. Pioneered a new modernism in the USA. Used clear, simple forms bordering on naivety. Chose unconventional subjects such as animal bones and urban architecture as well as the more usual mountains and flowers. Best known for semi-abstractions inspired by the bleak but colourful landscapes of Mexico.

Picasso, Pablo (1881–1973)

Spanish, but moved to France when he was 20. Co-founder of Cubism. Considered by many to be the greatest artist of the twentieth century as well as one of the most prolific artists ever. Painted scenes, objects and people as distorted and fragmented elements. Work was bold and full of energy and passion. Continued to work well into old age.

Pollock, Jackson (1912–1956)

American. One of the first exponents of Action Painting. Used to fix a very large canvas to the floor and throw or pour the paint, or use all sorts of implements to apply it. Also used sand, broken glass and other materials to give texture. Used emotion as his driving force. Often unhappy and struggled with a drink problem. Killed in a car crash at the age of 44.

Raeburn, Henry (1756–1823)

Scottish. One of Scotland's most popular artists. Painted the personalities of Edinburgh's Golden Age during the Enlightenment. Knighted by King George IV and, only a few months before his death, was appointed His Majesty's Limner for Scotland.

Ramsay, Allan (1713–1784)

Scottish, but worked mostly in London. One of the foremost portrait-painters of his time. Became the Court Painter to George III in 1760. Much influenced by contemporary French and Italian artists, but developed his own style of 'captivating charm and sensitivity'.

Raphael (1483–1520)

Italian. Considered to be one of the greatest draughtsmen of Western art. Leading artist at the court of Pope Julius II. Noted for the calm, serenity and simplicity of his paintings. Also a designer of sculpture and an architect. Very popular in his lifetime; even the Pope is reported to have cried when he died at the age of 37.

Rembrandt van Rijn (1606–1669)

Dutch. A great master of Baroque painting. Painted many self-portraits at different ages. Used light and shade to achieve emotional effects. In portraits, was able to express the character of his subject. In later life, produced many etchings, especially of Bible stories. Had a very sad life, with only one child outliving him. Achieved fame, good social standing and affluence but, after being widowed, was declared bankrupt and died in poverty.

Renoir, Pierre-Auguste (1841–1919)

French. One of the most popular Impressionists. Often portrayed people relaxing and enjoying themselves. Liked to paint outdoors and capture special effects of light, as did Monet, a close friend.

Riley, Bridget (1931–)

The leading British artist of Op Art (short for 'Optical Art'). Uses line and colour to create optical effects such as vibration, undulation and rotation in her huge paintings.

Ruysch, Rachel (1664–1750)

Dutch. One of the most successful still life painters at a time when there were few well-known woman artists. Specialized in floral arrangements, often with various insects, and was skilful at portraying the textures of petals and leaves and the way the light played on them.

Seurat, Georges (1859–1891)

French. Founder of Pointillism. Painted simple shapes with this technique, resulting in a sense of peace and stillness. Often painted scenes of people relaxing in the gardens of Paris and along the banks of the River Seine. Died of a severe infection at the age of 32.

Sutherland, Graham (1903–1980)

English. Best known for his portraits and religious art, especially his design for the giant tapestry in Coventry Cathedral. Also painted landscapes and was an official war artist. The realism of his portraits was not always appreciated by the sitters: Lady Churchill destroyed his portrait of the late Sir Winston Churchill because she disliked it intensely.

Turner, J M W (1775–1851)

English. Ahead of his time in that his landscapes tended towards the abstract with objects rarely having clearly defined outlines. Excelled in showing extremes of weather, e.g. rough seas, storms and blizzards. Able to capture unusual effects of light and movement, often in pale, luminous colours.

Warhol, Andy (1928–1987)

American. One of the twentieth century's best known Pop Artists. Often repeated an image across a canvas, rather like tiles — for example, soup cans or the face of Marilyn Monroe. Rebelled against much of the ethos surrounding art. Used print and photography to help achieve the final product he was looking for.

Notes

Notes

Notes

Have you seen these other NCEC resources for work with children?

Activity Clubs

The Paintbox Project is the latest of NCEC's Activity Clubs – annual themed collections of games, music, art and craft activities, cookery, story-telling, and worship ideas, designed for use at church groups, holiday clubs, youth groups and all-age events. Other Activity Clubs still available include:

All Aboard!

Draws together exciting activities based on the idea of a train journey, reflecting on the theme of faith journeys and pilgrimage. Material for six sessions, including a serialized story.

Plagues and Promises

Follow the fortunes of Moses as he travels from Egypt to the Promised Land. Bible-based activities, exploring the theme of community. There are six sessions, including all kinds of activities and a serialized drama.

Bible Exploration

Each year, NCEC publishes a themed set of Bible study material including a children's Workbook for 7–11-year-olds and a Study Guide suitable for leaders and adult groups. Workbooks feature a wide range of activities based on the Bible passages, and encourage children to build up a project folder. The Study Guides are an interactive resource for members of adult groups and youth groups, and leaders of all age-groups. They contain ideas and activities to help groups and individuals explore the material creatively, and include detailed study of the Bible passages and the historical context.

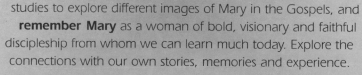

Remembering Mary

Mary plays an important part in the New Testament, as the one who holds in her memory many of the most significant events in the drama of the incarnation. Use these studies to explore different images of Mary in the Gospels, and **remember Mary** as a woman of bold, visionary and faithful discipleship from whom we can learn much today. Explore the connections with our own stories, memories and experience.

Angles on Jesus

This material focuses on Mark's Gospel. It looks at the different aspects of Jesus' character and ministry as revealed in the stories. Explorers are challenged to examine their own views and preconceptions of Jesus. There are five sections: *Risktaker, Rulebreaker, Riddle-teller, Role-reverser* and *Reject*.

For further information or to place an order, please contact:
National Christian Education Council, 1020 Bristol Road, Selly Oak, Birmingham B29 6LB.
Tel: 0121 472 4242   *Fax:* 0121 472 7575
E-mail: sales@ncec.org.uk   *Web site:* www.ncec.org.uk